What's Cooking, Alaska?

100 Recipes from Alaska's Favorite Chef

Chef Al Levinsohn
with Jody Ellis-Knapp

SASQUATCH BOOKS
SEATTLE

Cooking is an art form—an expression of the soul. This book is dedicated to all who strive to please the ones they love through their expression of food. To all of you, *bon appétit.*

Printed in Canada
Published by Sasquatch Books
Distributed by PGW/Perseus
15 14 13 12 11 10 09 08   9 8 7 6 5 4 3 2 1

Chef Al photograph: David Belisle
Landscape photograph: Jeremy Sauskojus/Stock.Xchng
Cover design: Rosebud Eustace
Interior design and composition: Rosebud Eustace
Food photography: Diane Padys
Food styling: Patty Wittmann
Prop styling: Cynthia Verner

Library of Congress Cataloging-in-Publication Data

Levinsohn, Al.
   What's cooking, Alaska? : 100 recipes from Alaska's favorite chef / Al Levinsohn
with Jody Ellis-Knapp.
      p. cm.
   Includes index.
    ISBN-13: 978-1-57061-549-8
    ISBN-10: 1-57061-549-7
    1. Cookery, American. 2. Cookery--Alaska. I. Ellis-Knapp, Jody. II. Title.

TX715.L65987 2008
641.59798--dc22

                      2007047687

Sasquatch Books
119 South Main Street, Suite 400
Seattle, WA 98104
(206) 467-4300
www.sasquatchbooks.com
custserv@sasquatchbooks.com

Contents

There is no love sincerer than the love of food.
—George Bernard Shaw

||||||||||||||||||||||||||||||||||||||||||||||||||||||||||||||||||||||||||||||||||||||||||||||||||||||||||||||||

Introduction

Food has always been an artistic endeavor for me. I cannot think of a better way to bring people together than by serving a great meal. Seeing the pleasure on their faces as they try a new dish is the ultimate reward and gives me more personal satisfaction than any international accolade.

I have been involved in food and cooking for so long, it is difficult for me to remember a time when the kitchen was not a huge part of my life. I started working in Seattle-area hotels back in the seventies. My first job was as a dishwasher at Sea Galley restaurant when I was sixteen years old. Even at sixteen, I was entranced with the industry and found it exciting. One of my high school classes required that we write a paper about our after-school jobs—a paper that, for me, turned out to foretell my future as a chef. In that paper, my ambitions were clear and precise. I wrote about how important it was to be "alert, quick, and efficient" when working in a restaurant. I effused over my $3.45 per hour wage as a dishwasher, stating that while I knew it wasn't enough pay to live on, I hoped to move up quickly in the industry.

Perhaps the most telling paragraph of this paper foreshadows things to come and shows the heart of my interest in food:

I help prepare and set up the salad bar, and quite often I help the cooks in preparing the seafood and sometimes

even in cooking it. This is what I really would like to do—
learn to be a cook. I have obtained a lot of knowledge and
experience in preparing food and hopefully I will be able
to advance to a cook one of these days, or at least be able
to work in food preparation and not just wash dishes.

Even then, my eyes were on Alaska, where I'd spent summers working and visiting family. That high school paper closed with the statement that I did not know what my lifetime ambitions might be, but that I hoped to return to Alaska after graduation and live there. It is amazing how accurate that paper, written so many years ago, turned out to be.

This brash confidence that only a sixteen-year-old can have helped me into my first sous-chef position at age eighteen, and it seems that it all just took off from there. I eventually realized my dream of making my way to Alaska, finding a place of rugged beauty and friendly people. What a wonderful state to call home!

Over the years, many chefs have mentored me and guided me toward the success I enjoy today. I especially admire Jens Haagen Hansen, owner of Jens' Restaurant in Anchorage, for his contin-ued passion for cooking. I worked under Jens in the early eight-ies when he was the head chef at the Crow's Nest Restaurant, also in Anchorage. A lot of my passion for food stems from his zeal and enthusiasm.

My food philosophy is about simplicity and separation of flavors and textures. I believe it is more important to focus on cooking the food correctly than making things too complex. Keep it sim-ple! This method allows the flavor of the foods to come through in every meal.

What's Cooking, Alaska? is a collection of the recipes I have created over the years. Many have been showcased on my cook-ing show, *What's Cookin'? with Chef Al*, which airs every week on Anchorage's local KTUU channel 2. Other recipes have been used in my restaurants. The recipes in this book are very user-friendly and relatively simple. When preparing them, think about what flavors or accompaniments you think would complement the dish.

Don't be afraid to experiment! Get creative and make these dishes your own. If a recipe calls for pork, try chicken. If it calls for halibut, use salmon instead.

Good food, good friends, and good times. These are the ultimate ingredients for any successful meal. Make them a priority in your kitchen. And have fun—cooking is what you make of it, and good cooking is finding enjoyment in your creation.

Appetizers

Mama Wags' Mighty Molten Crab Artichoke Dip

King Crab Cakes

Quick Oysters Rockefeller

Oysters Casino

Kodiak Scallop Wontons

Ale-Battered Halibut with City Diner Tartar Sauce

Southern-Style Halibut Fritters

Alaskan Snapper Ceviche

Russian River Red Salmon Lox

Smoked Alaskan Salmon Bruschetta

Wild and Wonderful Beef Tartare

Kincaid Grill's Gorgonzola Fondue

Kachemak Bay Steamed Mussels with Fresh Herbs

Taste of New Orleans Barbecue Shrimp

The appetite is sharpened by the first bites.
—José Rizal

LET'S GET THIS PARTY STARTED! The right appetizers can be the perfect launching pad for your entertaining, setting the mood and style of your party or private dinner.

Appetizers have a long and colorful history. The Romans would serve a large assortment of small dishes before their banquets, including eggs, mushrooms, and cheeses. In the Middle East, the Arabs were known for their *maza*, abundant starters that served as a precursor to their equally abundant meals. It is believed that the Arabs carried the tradition to the Iberian Peninsula during the nine hundred years they inhabited that part of Europe and that it was the early inspiration for Spanish tapas. Tapas continue to be an important part of Spanish cuisine and the local custom of gathering before dinner to enjoy drinks, food, and good conversation.

Then there are hors d'oeuvres, a term coined in Paris in the 1600s and used to describe dishes intended as a supplement to the first or second course of a meal.

Alaska might not have a specific regional name for its appetizers, but no matter what you call them—hors d'oeuvres, *maza*, tapas, or just plain starters—it is apparent that they are the touchstone of any great meal or party.

These appetizer recipes are some of my favorites and highlight the freshest ingredients and Alaskan seafood at its finest.

Mama Wags' Mighty Molten Crab Artichoke Dip

Makes 6 servings

This recipe is a takeoff on a classic Christmas Eve recipe. My Aunt Joann Wagner, or "Mama Wags" as we call her, used to make this for us every holiday at her Anchorage hillside home. My addition of crab and cilantro gives it a whole new twist. Don't tell her I changed it up a bit!

1 cup sour cream

1 cup mayonnaise

⅓ cup diced green chiles

1 cup grated Parmesan cheese (8 ounces)

1 cup diced artichoke hearts

2 tablespoons chopped fresh cilantro

1 pound cooked crabmeat, excess moisture squeezed out and patted dry

Preheat the oven to 375°F.

In a medium-size mixing bowl, combine the sour cream, mayonnaise, green chiles, Parmesan, artichoke hearts, and cilantro. Gently fold in the crabmeat. Be careful not to break up the chunks of crab too much. Spoon the mixture into a lightly greased 9- by 9-inch baking dish.

Bake in the oven for 15 to 20 minutes, or until the dip is brown and bubbly. Serve immediately.

King Crab Cakes

Makes 4 to 6 servings

It might be considered the "deadliest catch," but Alaskan king crab is beyond compare in richness and taste. This is the number-one signature dish of Kincaid Grill, popular from the day we opened. I use cream cheese because it gives the cakes a very light and airy texture.

> ¼ cup equal parts finely diced red, yellow, and green bell peppers
>
> ¼ cup equal parts finely diced celery, carrot, and red onion
>
> ¾ pound cooked king crabmeat, excess water squeezed out and patted dry
>
> ¼ cup mayonnaise
>
> ¼ cup (2 ounces) whipped cream cheese
>
> 1 tablespoon chopped fresh parsley
>
> 1 teaspoon chopped fresh dill
>
> 1 cup all-purpose flour
>
> 1 egg, beaten
>
> 1 cup panko-style bread crumbs
>
> 2 tablespoons vegetable oil

Lightly coat a small skillet with cooking spray and heat to medium heat. Cook the bell peppers, celery, carrot, and onion until they are crisp-tender, stirring. Wipe down the skillet for later use. Spread the vegetables on a baking sheet and let cool. Once completely cooled, remove to a medium-size bowl. Wipe down the baking sheet for later use.

Using a wooden spoon, combine the vegetables, crabmeat, mayonnaise, cream cheese, parsley, and dill. Shape the mixture by hand into about 10 or 12 cakes and put them on the baking sheet. Cover with plastic wrap and place the cakes in the freezer until firm but not frozen (about 45 minutes).

Remove the crab cakes from the freezer and dredge them in flour, shaking off any excess. Dip the crab cakes in the egg, then toss them in bread crumbs until completely coated.

Heat the vegetable oil in the skillet over medium heat. Fry the crab cakes until golden brown, about 2 minutes on each side. Serve with your choice of dipping sauce.

Quick Oysters Rockefeller

Makes 2 to 4 servings

I love oysters Rockefeller. This classic, simple recipe is named for its "richness." Alaskan oysters are renowned as being some of the most flavorful in the world, and this recipe really brings out that wealth of taste in half the time of other recipes. You can substitute light cream cheese and low-fat sour cream for a more heart-healthy dish.

1 dozen oysters, shucked and on the half shell

Approximately ½ cup rock salt

¼ cup (2 ounces) soft cream cheese

¼ cup sour cream

½ cup thawed frozen chopped spinach, drained and patted dry

¼ cup grated Parmesan cheese (2 ounces)

Kosher salt and white pepper

½ cup fresh bread crumbs

2 tablespoons unsalted butter, melted

To shuck an oyster: Hold the oyster in a towel. Finding the slight indent in the tip of the oyster, carefully insert the point of an oyster knife at a 45 degree angle. Twist the knife in a back and forth motion while applying pressure. As the knife penetrates into the oyster, give a final full twist to pop the oyster open. Apply pressure to the top of the shell to cut the oyster free. Slide the knife point under the oyster to loosen, keeping the water intact. Be sure to remove any remaining small bits of shell.

Preheat the oven to 375°F.

Line an oven-safe dish with rock salt and place the oysters in it. This helps keep them upright so they retain the natural moisture in the shell.

In a medium-size bowl, combine the cream cheese, sour cream, spinach, and Parmesan. Season with salt and pepper to taste. Top each oyster with a dollop of the mixture. Combine the bread crumbs and butter in a small bowl, then sprinkle that on top of cream cheese mixture.

Bake in the center of the oven until brown and slightly bubbly, about 8 to 10 minutes. Serve immediately.

Oysters Casino

Makes 6 to 8 servings

Rumor has it that this recipe was originally developed at a casino in the Hamptons on Long Island, New York. This version is another personal favorite of mine, and I think our Alaskan oysters give it an extra boost! The combination of the fresh vegetables, cheese, garlic, and bacon really complement the succulent flavor of the oysters. This recipe also works great with clams and mussels.

¼ cup (½ stick) unsalted butter, softened

1 tablespoon minced shallot

1 tablespoon minced garlic

¼ cup minced celery

¼ cup minced green bell pepper

¼ cup grated Parmesan cheese

¼ cup plain bread crumbs

1½ tablespoons fresh lemon juice

2 tablespoons chopped fresh parsley

Kosher salt and freshly ground black pepper

Approximately 2 cups rock salt

2 dozen oysters, shucked and on the half shell (see recipe note on page 6)

4 cooked strips of bacon (cooked very lightly, not crisp), broken into 24 pieces

Preheat the oven to 450°F.

In a medium-size saucepan, melt the butter over low heat. Cook the shallots, garlic, celery, and green pepper over low heat until tender, about 5 to 7 minutes. Remove from the heat and stir in the Parmesan, bread crumbs, lemon juice, and parsley. Season with kosher salt and pepper to taste.

Line the bottom of a large baking dish with rock salt, about ½ inch deep. Place the oysters on the rock salt to keep them upright and retain the natural moisture in the shell. Divide the shallots-garlic mixture evenly over the oysters. Top each with a square of bacon. Bake in the center of the oven for 5 to 7 minutes, or until the bacon is crisp. Serve hot!

Kodiak Scallop Wontons

Makes 6 to 8 servings

I spent some time working in Hong Kong in the early nineties, and that influence still carries through in my cooking. Many of my favorite recipes have Asian-fusion flair, and this one really highlights the combination of Alaska seafood and Far East cuisine. This recipe has a really nice texture and crunch, thanks to the cabbage in the wontons. The garlic and ginger make for a very aromatic and flavorful appetizer.

1 tablespoon olive oil

½ cup diced green cabbage

¼ cup diced yellow onion

½ tablespoon minced garlic

1 tablespoon minced peeled ginger

½ teaspoon freshly ground black pepper

½ cup diced fresh shiitake mushrooms

1 pound large Kodiak scallops (approximately 10), rinsed and patted dry

15 to 20 wonton wrappers (use as many as needed)

1 egg, beaten

Preheat the oven to 375°F.

Heat the olive oil in a skillet over medium heat. Cook the cabbage, onions, garlic, ginger, and pepper until just tender, stirring for about 2 to 3 minutes. Fold in the mushrooms and remove from the heat.

In a food processor or blender, puree the scallops until they are a smooth paste. Fold the scallops into the vegetables.

Spoon roughly 1 tablespoon of the mixture into each wonton wrapper. Fold the edges together and gently press to seal. Brush the top of each wonton lightly with the egg. Bake for 10 to 12 minutes, or until golden. Serve immediately with your favorite dipping sauce.

Ale-Battered Halibut
with City Diner Tartar Sauce

Makes 6 servings

You can find beer-battered halibut in just about any restaurant in Anchorage. This recipe has no eggs, which makes it unusual. With the elimination of heavy breading, it has a crispy finish that does not overwhelm the fish. Dip the finished halibut in some City Diner Tartar Sauce and enjoy!

Canola oil, 4 inches deep in fryer or skillet

1 cup all-purpose flour (reserve 1 tablespoon for dusting the fish)

1 cup cornstarch

1 teaspoon baking powder

½ teaspoon granulated sugar

1 teaspoon kosher salt

One 16-ounce bottle Alaskan Amber ale (or any beer)

1 pound halibut (or any fish), skinned and boned, cut into 1-inch cubes

City Diner Tartar Sauce (recipe follows)

Heat the canola oil in a deep-fryer or large skillet to 350°F.

In a medium-size bowl, combine the flour, cornstarch, baking powder, sugar, and salt. Pour in the ale and mix well with a wire whisk, until the consistency is like that of cake batter.

Lightly dust the halibut pieces with the reserved flour. Dip them in the batter and place immediately into the deep-fryer. Cook until golden brown, about 5 to 7 minutes. Serve immediately with the tartar sauce.

City Diner Tartar Sauce

2 cups mayonnaise

½ cup dill pickle relish

Juice of 2 lemons (about ¼ cup)

1 teaspoon Tabasco sauce

¼ cup minced onion

½ tablespoon garlic powder

1 tablespoon dried parsley

1 tablespoon chopped capers

1 tablespoon dried dill

In a medium-size bowl, combine the mayonnaise, relish, lemon juice, Tabasco sauce, onion, garlic, parsley, capers, and dill. Using a wooden spoon, mix well.

Store the tartar sauce in an airtight container in the refrigerator until ready to use, or up to 1 week.

Southern-Style Halibut Fritters

Makes 6 to 8 servings

I grew up eating corn fritters. My dad would make them for us on a regular basis and we would devour them. He wouldn't fully approve of my version of fritters, as he doesn't much care for seafood of any kind! I urge you to try this recipe, as you will be astounded at the flavor the halibut adds to these wonderful little bites.

> **Canola or vegetable oil, 4 inches deep in skillet**
>
> **1 cup all-purpose flour**
>
> **1 tablespoon baking powder**
>
> **¼ teaspoon salt**
>
> **¼ teaspoon freshly ground white pepper**
>
> **½ pound halibut, finely diced**
>
> **6 ounces clam juice**
>
> **½ cup milk**

Heat the canola oil in a large skillet to 375°F, or until it has a slight haze.

In a small bowl, combine the flour, baking powder, salt, and pepper and set aside. Put the halibut, clam juice, and milk in a large bowl. Incorporate the dry ingredients into the wet, mixing well by hand. Drop the mixture by spoonfuls into the skillet and fry until golden brown, about 5 to 7 minutes.

Serve the fritters right away with your favorite dipping sauce.

Alaskan Snapper Ceviche

Makes 6 to 8 servings

I found from personal experience that this recipe works great when you are out on a fishing charter and all you have are the ingredients for sandwiches and margaritas! Use red snapper or your catch of the day and enjoy a floating fiesta while fishing the afternoon away. Garnish with grapefruit sections, avocado slices, and tortilla chips.

Juice of 2 grapefruits (about 1 cup)

Juice of 1 lime (about 2 tablespoons)

¼ cup tequila

1 red snapper fillet (about 2 pounds), cut into 1-inch pieces and bones removed

2 tablespoons olive oil

½ bunch cilantro, chopped

1 medium red bell pepper, chopped

1 medium orange bell pepper, chopped

1 medium red onion, cut into ¼-inch-thick slices

Kosher salt and freshly ground black pepper

Pour the grapefruit juice, lime juice, and tequila into a mixing bowl. Toss in the red snapper pieces and marinate in the refrigerator for at least 5 hours.

Discard the marinade and stir in the olive oil, cilantro, red pepper, orange pepper, and onion. Season with salt and pepper to taste.

Serve in martini glasses or small bowls, garnishing with grapefruit segments, avocado slices, and tortilla strips.

Russian River Red Salmon Lox

Makes 4 servings

Alaska's southern peninsula regularly yields trophy-size fish to avid anglers. The Russian River is often "combat fishing" at its finest, with fisherman standing shoulder to shoulder as they reel in their catches. You can almost walk across the fish during a run and you will quickly limit out. Returning home with two days' limit, you might wonder what to do with all that fish! Red salmon works exceptionally well in this Scandinavian-style dish. Enjoy it with the Brown Sugar–Dill Sauce, first introduced to me by my crazy Danish friend Jens Hansen back in the eighties when we worked at the Crow's Nest Restaurant.

> ½ cup kosher salt
>
> 1 cup granulated sugar
>
> ½ cup freshly ground black pepper
>
> ½ cup chopped fresh dill
>
> ½ cup vodka
>
> 1 red salmon fillet (2 to 3 pounds), scaled and boned
>
> Brown Sugar–Dill Sauce (recipe follows)

Mix together the salt, sugar, pepper, dill, and vodka in a small bowl. Rub the mixture over the flesh side of the salmon.

Wrap the fish tightly in plastic wrap and place it in a deep casserole. Place another pan on top of the fish, with a weight in it to keep the pressure on the salmon. Refrigerate for 24 hours, then turn the fish and refrigerate for another 12 hours.

Remove the salmon from the refrigerator and cut the fish into thin slices, serving with Brown Sugar–Dill Sauce.

Brown Sugar-Dill Sauce

1 cup firmly packed brown sugar

¼ cup Dijon mustard

¼ cup water

2 tablespoons chopped fresh dill

In a small saucepan, combine the brown sugar, mustard, and water. Bring the mixture to a boil. Allow it to reduce by 30 percent or so (this should take about 5 minutes). Remove from the heat and stir in the dill.

Serve the sauce at room temperature or slightly chilled. Can be stored in the refrigerator for up to 2 weeks.

Smoked Alaskan Salmon Bruschetta

Makes 8 to 10 servings

Over the course of a summer, we Alaskans put away our fair share of smoked salmon. Trying to find a new and unique presentation can be a challenge, as one gets tired of salmon dips and spreads. This is a great way to utilize smoked salmon or any smoked fish.

½ cup smoked silver salmon, flaked

1¼ cups diced tomatoes

½ cup chopped fresh basil

¼ cup crumbled feta cheese

French baguette, cut into 2 dozen ½-inch-thick diagonal slices

½ cup olive oil

Preheat the oven to 400°F.

In a small bowl, combine the salmon, tomatoes, basil, and feta. Set aside.

Brush the baguette slices with olive oil on both sides. Put the bread on a baking sheet and toast in the center of the oven for about 5 to 7 minutes, until the slices are well browned and crisp. Remove from the oven and let them cool to room temperature.

Top each toast slice with the salmon mixture. Serve immediately.

Wild and Wonderful Beef Tartare

Makes 4 servings

Using a good cut of beef is the secret to creating a beef tartare that is fresh and flavorful. This recipe will make even those who like their meat well-done change their minds on the idea of "raw" food. I like to serve this at small dinner parties or enjoy it with a salad for lunch.

½ pound trimmed filet mignon

2 tablespoons capers

1 tablespoon chopped parsley

¼ cup minced white onion

1 tablespoon Worcestershire sauce

1 egg yolk (optional)

Salt and freshly ground black pepper

4 slices toasted bread, crust removed, cut into points

Using a chef's knife, chop the beef by hand until very fine. In a medium-size bowl, combine the beef, capers, parsley, onion, Worcestershire sauce (to taste), and egg yolk. Season with salt and pepper to taste.

Remove the mixture to a platter and serve with toast points. Garnish with additional parsley.

Kincaid Grill's Gorgonzola Fondue

Makes 6 to 8 servings

This appetizer is a signature dish at the Kincaid Grill. Fondues have started to make a comeback and have become increasingly popular. I've found a slightly different twist with the Gorgonzola, and it has made this fondue a favorite among my restaurant patrons. It works equally well for small dinner parties or large gatherings. Serve it with French bread, crackers, bruschetta, or fresh fruits.

One 8-ounce package regular cream cheese (1 cup)

¾ cup crumbled Gorgonzola cheese

¼ cup grated Parmesan cheese (2 ounces)

½ cup heavy cream

¼ cup chopped roasted garlic (see recipe note below)

2 tablespoons white wine

To roast garlic: Preheat the oven to 400°F. Slightly trim the top of a garlic bulb and put it on a sheet of aluminum foil. Drizzle with olive oil and seal the foil to form a packet. Bake in the center of the oven until the garlic is tender, about 30 minutes, depending on how much garlic you roast. Let cool and store in an airtight container in the refrigerator until ready to use, or up to 1 week.

Preheat the oven to 400°F.

Combine all the ingredients in a mixer fitted with a paddle until well blended, about 3 minutes. Scoop the mixture into a shallow glass dish and bake for 15 to 20 minutes, or until brown and bubbly. Serve immediately.

Kachemak Bay Steamed Mussels with Fresh Herbs

Makes 4 servings

Just off the coast of the fishing town of Homer, Alaska, is the beauty that is Kachemak Bay. Amazing mountains rise up against the sky and wildlife is abundant, but fresh seafood is the bounty most enjoyed by all. I prefer this recipe for its simplicity. There is no better way to get the flavors of the ocean than with this combination of fresh mussels and herbs from the garden.

¼ cup olive oil

2 tablespoons minced shallot

2 tablespoons minced garlic

4 ounces andouille sausage, cut into ½-inch pieces

1 pound Pacific mussels, scrubbed and debearded
   (discard any open mussels)

½ cup white wine

½ cup diced fresh tomatoes

¼ cup (½ stick) unsalted butter

¼ cup chopped fresh herbs (equal parts oregano, thyme, basil,
   and parsley)

2 tablespoons fresh lemon juice

Salt and freshly ground black pepper

Heat the olive oil in a large saucepan over medium heat. Cook the shallots, garlic, and sausage, stirring until heated through. Add the mussels and white wine. Cover and cook until the mussels open, about 2 to 3 minutes. Stir in the tomatoes, butter, herbs, and lemon juice, tossing to combine.

Season to taste with salt and pepper. Serve immediately in shallow bowls. Ladle some broth over each serving.

Taste of New Orleans Barbecue Shrimp

Makes 4 servings

This recipe is one of the best seafood appetizers I have ever created. Different from classic barbecue, it has that New Orleans kick and will make you feel as though you are partying at Mardi Gras! The sauce is equally good on any seafood—try it with salmon or halibut.

½ cup (1 stick) unsalted butter

½ cup olive oil

½ cup chili sauce

1½ tablespoons Worcestershire sauce

2 teaspoons minced garlic

1 teaspoon chopped parsley

1 teaspoon dried oregano

1 teaspoon cayenne pepper

½ teaspoon Tabasco sauce

1½ tablespoons liquid smoke

¾ teaspoon kosher salt

¾ teaspoon freshly ground black pepper

2 pounds Alaska spot shrimp

Preheat the oven to 400°F.

Combine all the ingredients except the shrimp. Cook over low heat in a double boiler, whisking often until the butter is melted and all ingredients are well incorporated—do not overheat or boil.

Add the shrimp and gently toss until they are coated. Spread the shrimp in a single layer on a large baking sheet, then place in the oven and roast for 6 to 8 minutes, or until they are heated through and slightly charred.

Soups and Salads

Basic Stocks

Rich and Creamy Roasted Onion Soup with King Crab Croutons

Classic Onion Soup

Mat Valley Corn Chowder

Perfect Potato Leek Soup

"Sandwich in a Bowl" (aka Bacon, Lettuce, and Tomato Soup)

Venison Red Chili with Cilantro Onion Relish

City Diner–Style Chili with Beans

Thai Chicken Chili, Alaskan Style

Forest Mushroom Soup with Kodiak Scallops

Midnight Sun Oyster Stew

Ocean Fresh Seafood Gumbo

Kincaid Grill's Seafood Fusion

Deckhand's Seafood Cioppino

Cream of Butternut Squash Soup

Thai-Style Cabbage Wraps

Traditional Caesar Salad

Poached Pear Salad with Fireweed Honey–Pepper Vinaigrette

From-the-Sea Shellfish Salad

Kincaid Grill's Scallop Niçoise

Grilled Spot Shrimp Salad

Poached Alaskan Salmon Salad with Mustard Vinaigrette

Pioneer Peak Potato Pancake Salad with Smoked Salmon and
White Truffle Vinaigrette

Only the pure of heart can make good soup.
—LUDWIG VAN BEETHOVEN

IN SOUTH-CENTRAL ALASKA, we don't have the growing season for salad fixings that the "Lower 48" (what we call the continental United States) does. But that doesn't dissuade gardeners from cultivating a bounty of fresh vegetables each season. You will see lettuce being grown in window planters, zucchinis as big as my arm, and cabbages that look like they came from outer space! We tend to do everything to extremes here in the last frontier, so it is no surprise that despite a limited season, our vegetables are some of the best around. With my philosophy of always using the freshest possible ingredients, I try to incorporate as much local produce as I can into my soups and salads.

Our short summers also mean that people don't always want to spend a lot of time in the kitchen—we are too busy enjoying the outdoors and the endless daylight. Soups and salads are a perfect alternative to a heavy meal, especially on a hot day when the last thing anyone wants to do is cook over a hot stove or grill.

As always, I've created these dishes with simplicity in mind. Pure flavors and fresh foods make for the best meals. Whether you use these recipes to present an impressive initial course at a dinner party or to serve up as a main meal at a casual family dinner, you'll be sure to enjoy both the preparation and the results.

Basic Stocks

Keeping a good stock on hand is important for any cook's kitchen. Here are my recipes for basic chicken, fish, beef, and veal stocks. Make your stock ahead of time and freeze in an airtight container for later use. Chicken and fish stocks will last up to 1 year if stored properly; beef and veal stocks will remain good for several months.

Chicken Stock

> **5 pounds chicken bones**
>
> **2 tablespoons unsalted butter**
>
> **1 medium yellow onion, coarsely chopped**
>
> **1 medium carrot, coarsely chopped**
>
> **1 stalk celery, coarsely chopped**
>
> **12 cups (3 quarts) cold water**

Rinse the bones under running cold water for 10 minutes. The bones should be as fresh as possible. Melt the butter over medium heat in a large stockpot. Add the onion, carrot, and celery and cook for about 5 minutes. Toss in the bones and pour in the cold water.

Allow the stock to simmer, uncovered, for at least 4 hours, skimming the fat off the top every so often with a spoon. Strain the stock through a fine strainer. Let cool to room temperature and store in an airtight container in the refrigerator or freezer until ready to use. Stock will keep in the refrigerator for up to 1 week and in the freezer for up to 1 year.

(continued)

Fish Stock

5 pounds fish bones (halibut, sole, or flounder are perfect)

2 tablespoons unsalted butter

1 medium yellow onion, coarsely chopped

1 medium carrot, coarsely chopped

1 stalk celery, coarsely chopped

1 bunch leeks (green part only), rinsed and chopped

4 ounces fennel branches, trimmed

2 cloves garlic, peeled and left whole

12 cups (3 quarts) cold water

2 cups dry white wine

1 bouquet garni (see recipe note below)

*A bouquet garni is a bundle of fresh herbs—such as bay
leaf, parsley, thyme, and tarragon branches—tied in cheesecloth and
used to flavor soups, stocks, and stews.*

Rinse the fish bones under cold running water for 10 minutes. Make sure the bones are as fresh as possible. Melt the butter over medium heat in a large stockpot. Stir in the onion, carrot, celery, leeks, fennel, and garlic and cook for about 5 minutes. Toss in the fish bones and cook for about 40 minutes, or until the bones turn white and the mixture begins to smell appetizing. Pour in the cold water and the wine. Gently bring the mixture to a simmer.

Allow the stock to simmer for 1 to 2 hours, uncovered, skimming the fat off the top with a spoon every now and then. Strain through a fine strainer. Let cool to room temperature before storing. Fish stock should be used the same day it is made or stored in an airtight container in the freezer for up to 1 year.

Beef or Veal Stock (Demi-Glace)

5 pounds beef or veal bones, split

2 medium yellow onions, coarsely chopped

2 medium carrots, coarsely chopped

1 stalk celery, coarsely chopped

1 cup tomato paste

32 cups (8 quarts) cold water

Preheat the oven to 400°F.

Brown the bones in a roasting pan in the oven, turning occasionally until they are well browned. Remove the bones and place in a large stockpot. Deglaze the roasting pan with some of the water to loosen up the juices, adding this to the stockpot.

In a separate pan, sauté the vegetables until they are caramelized, about 10 minutes. Add the tomato paste to the vegetables. Put the vegetable mixture and cold water in the stockpot. Bring the mixture to a simmer (do not boil). Simmer on low heat for 24 to 30 hours, skimming occasionally. Strain through a sieve, pressing the bones and vegetables against the mesh to get full flavor.

Pour the liquid back into pot and begin reducing over medium heat. The liquid will begin to take on a velvety consistency and is considered done when it just coats the back of a spoon. At this point, strain again through a fine sieve, let cool, and store for later use.

Beef or veal stock can be stored in the refrigerator for up to 1 week. Alternatively, allow it to cool until gelled and store in resealable plastic bags in the freezer for several months.

Rich and Creamy Roasted Onion Soup
with King Crab Croutons

Makes 8 servings

Roasted onions add a sweet flavor to any dish. I developed this recipe when I was making regular onion soup and didn't like the way it was splashing around in the bowls. I wondered about creating a soup that was thicker and heartier, more of a meal. I dusted the caramelized onions with flour and added some cream, and voila! A beautiful, rich soup.

2 cups diced yellow onion

½ cup (1 stick) unsalted butter

¼ cup minced shallot

¾ cup all-purpose flour

5 cups chicken stock, warmed (see Basic Stocks on page 25)

1 cup half-and-half or heavy cream

½ cup sherry

1 tablespoon chopped fresh thyme

Kosher salt and freshly ground white pepper

In a 4-quart stockpot over medium heat, cook the onions, stirring occasionally for about 10 minutes, until they have a nice brown color and begin to caramelize. Stir in the butter and shallot, cooking until tender, about 3 minutes. Mix in the flour, stirring with a spoon until a smooth roux forms.

Continue cooking over low heat until the roux achieves a sheen to it, then pour in the chicken stock and bring to a light boil. Stir vigorously for about 5 minutes, until the mixture reaches a smooth consistency. Cook over low heat until the flour taste is gone, about 30 to 45 minutes. Pour in the half-and-half and sherry. Stir in the thyme and season to taste with salt and pepper.

If the soup is too thick, thin it with a little chicken stock. Strain the soup through a fine strainer, pressing the onion pieces against the strainer to remove their entire flavor. Discard solids. Keep the soup warm on low heat until ready to serve.

King Crab Croutons

1 baguette, cut into ½-inch slices (approximately 16 slices)

1 cup grated extra-sharp white cheddar cheese

1 cup king crabmeat, excess moisture squeezed out and patted dry

2 ounces bacon, cooked crisp and minced

1 tablespoon minced chives or green onion

Preheat the oven to 350°F.

Place the baguette slices on a large baking sheet and toast them until they are golden brown, about 7 minutes. Remove and let cool.

In a food processor fitted with a steel blade, process the cheddar until it forms a fine mince (do not overprocess). Add the crabmeat and pulse until just combined. Remove the mixture to a large bowl and fold in the bacon and chives or green onion.

Top each crouton with the cheese mixture and return it to the 350°F oven, heating until the cheese is bubbly, about 5 minutes. Serve immediately, or refrigerate for up to 3 days and reheat when needed.

Classic Onion Soup

Makes 2 to 3 servings

This recipe shares some similarities with the Rich and Creamy Roasted Onion Soup (see page 28), but it is the classic version for a more traditional style. Top individual oven-safe serving bowls with shredded Gruyère cheese and croutons, and heat under a broiler until bubbling.

¼ cup (½ stick) unsalted butter

2 cups yellow onions, cut into ¼-inch-thick slices

½ cup sherry

¼ cup minced shallot

3 cups chicken stock, warmed (see Basic Stocks on page 25)

½ tablespoon chopped fresh thyme

Kosher salt and freshly ground white pepper

In a large stockpot over medium heat, melt the butter. Cook the onions for about 45 minutes, stirring occasionally until they caramelize. Deglaze with the sherry, scraping any brown bits up from the bottom of the stockpot. Stir in the shallot, chicken stock, and thyme.

Season with salt and pepper to taste. Keep on low heat until ready to serve.

Mat Valley Corn Chowder

Makes 6 to 8 servings

The Matanuska-Susitna Valley is the heartland for Alaska's farming communities. Casually known as "the Valley," it still is home to working farms that provide local restaurants with fresh veggies and fruits. This recipe reminds me of the fresh taste of home-grown vegetables, Alaskan grown and harvested.

½ pound bacon, cut into ¼-inch slices

¼ cup minced yellow onion

¼ cup minced celery

½ cup (1 stick) unsalted butter

¾ cup all-purpose flour

1½ quarts (6 cups) chicken stock (see Basic Stocks on page 25)

One 17-ounce can (about 3 cups) creamed corn

2 cups diced cooked potatoes

½ cup diced roasted red bell pepper

1 tablespoon ground cumin

1 tablespoon garlic powder

1 teaspoon freshly ground white pepper

Heavy cream

Chopped fresh cilantro

Cook the bacon in a large skillet over medium-high heat until crisp. Cook the onion and celery in the bacon fat for about 3 to 5 minutes, stirring until tender. Stir in the butter and flour, mixing well to form a roux. Pour in the chicken stock and creamed corn. Whisk to combine, and cook over low heat until the flour taste is gone, about 30 minutes. Stir in the potato, red pepper, cumin, garlic powder, and white pepper.

Adjust to the desired thickness by adding more chicken stock. Pour in a splash of heavy cream to taste. Garnish with chopped crisp bacon and cilantro.

Perfect Potato Leek Soup

Makes 8 servings

Potatoes always remind me of crisp fall days and changing leaves. I first prepared this soup for my German friend and former boss, Chris. He loved it, and it has gone on to become an important part of my collection. It quickly becomes a favorite of all who try it. This soup has a classy style, yet is easy to make. Serve with a garnish of flaked smoked salmon, crisp bacon bits, and sour cream, or julienne of prosciutto with shaved Parmesan for a truly elegant touch.

½ cup (1 stick) unsalted butter

1 leek, rinsed and coarsely chopped (about 1 cup)

¼ cup finely diced celery

¼ cup finely diced yellow onion

¾ cup all-purpose flour

1½ quarts (6 cups) chicken stock, warmed (see Basic Stocks on page 25)

2 cups diced parboiled potatoes

1 cup half-and-half or heavy cream

1 tablespoon chopped fresh thyme

Kosher salt and freshly ground white pepper

Melt the butter in a large stockpot over medium heat. Cook the leek, celery, and onion for about 10 minutes, stirring until tender. Mix in the flour with a wooden spoon, creating a smooth roux, cooking over low heat until it develops a light sheen.

Pour in the chicken stock and bring to a boil, stirring vigorously for a few minutes to form a smooth consistency. Toss in the potatoes and lower the heat, cooking for about 30 minutes, or until the flour taste is gone. Stir in the half-and-half and thyme.

Season with salt and pepper to taste and serve immediately in warmed bowls.

"Sandwich in a Bowl"
(aka Bacon, Lettuce, and Tomato Soup)

Makes 6 servings

Having to create a unique daily soup at a restaurant can be difficult after awhile. I came up with this soup one day while making vegetable soup. I started out with the bacon, lettuce, and tomato ingredients. When I added the mayonnaise and croutons, it was just like eating a BLT sandwich! The cumin is the secret ingredient here, as it brings out the flavor of the bacon. Make it for the kids—they are sure to love it too!

½ cup diced yellow onion

½ cup diced green bell pepper

½ cup diced celery

One 19-ounce can diced tomatoes, undrained

2 quarts (8 cups) chicken stock (see Basic Stocks on page 25)

1 teaspoon ground cumin

1 pound bacon, cooked crisp and chopped

½ head iceberg lettuce, chopped into 1-inch pieces

Salt and freshly ground black pepper

Cook the onion, bell pepper, and celery in a large stockpot over medium-low heat until tender, about 5 minutes. Pour in the tomatoes. Bring the mixture to a simmer, then add the chicken stock and cumin. Simmer, uncovered, on low heat for 15 minutes. Stir in the bacon and lettuce.

Season to taste with salt and pepper. Top with croutons and a dollop of mayonnaise, serving immediately.

Venison Red Chili
with Cilantro Onion Relish

Makes 4 servings

It may not be common knowledge, but some areas of Alaska offer excellent deer hunting opportunities. Even if you are not a hunter, the rich, full flavor of venison will make this a favorite for family dinners or parties. This recipe also works wonderfully with moose meat, an Alaskan staple. If you don't happen to have a moose or deer available for hunting, regular beef works just fine too!

¼ cup clarified unsalted butter (see recipe note below)

2 pounds venison, cut into ¾-inch cubes

Salt and freshly ground black pepper

1 medium yellow onion, diced

2 to 3 tablespoons all-purpose flour

1 quart (4 cups) beef or chicken stock (see Basic Stocks on page 25)

1 cup Red Chile Paste (recipe follows)

Cilantro Onion Relish (recipe follows)

To clarify butter: Cook 1 pound of butter over low heat (a double boiler works well) until it turns clear on the top layer (about 30 to 40 minutes). Skim foam as required. It can be chilled and refrigerated for several days. When butter is clarified, it does not burn as easily as regular melted butter. This method allows you to separate and discard the milk solids.

Heat the butter in a large stockpot over medium-high heat. Season the venison with salt and pepper to taste, and brown until caramelized. Stir in the onion, cooking until translucent and tender, about 5 to 6 minutes. Mix in the flour to form a wet paste.

Pour in the stock and bring to a simmer. Whisk in the red chile paste to taste. Simmer, uncovered, over low heat for about 1½ to 2 hours, or until the meat is tender (a slow cooker works well at this point). Serve with the relish.

Red Chile Paste

8 to 10 medium New Mexico dried chiles

½ cup beef or chicken stock, heated (see Basic Stocks on page 25)

2 pasilla peppers (available at most grocery stores)

Break off the stems from the chiles and pour out the seeds (you might want to wear gloves). Soak the chiles in the hot stock until soft (about 10 minutes).

Roast the pasilla peppers over an open flame until charred, then peel, seed, and set aside. When the chiles are soft, combine them in a blender to form a smooth paste. Refrigerate the paste in an airtight container for up to 1 week.

Cilantro Onion Relish

½ cup red onion, minced

½ cup yellow onion, minced

¼ cup minced fresh cilantro

Juice of 1 lime (about 2 tablespoons)

Salt and freshly ground black pepper

In a medium-size bowl, combine the red onion, yellow onion, cilantro, and lime juice. Season with salt and pepper to taste. Let the mixture stand for 1 hour before serving to marry the flavors. Refrigerate the relish in an airtight container for up to 2 days.

City Diner-Style Chili with Beans

Makes 8 to 10 hearty servings

City Diner is a restaurant in midtown Anchorage that I co-own with my two good friends Jens and George. This recipe has that comfort food feel, which is the touchstone of City Diner itself. The great thing is, if you make it ahead and just let it simmer on a back burner of the stove or in a slow cooker all day, the flavors tend to get richer and denser, making it a timesaver as well as a tasty meal.

½ pound bacon, cut into ¼-inch-thick slices

2 cups diced white onion

12 cloves garlic, peeled and crushed

2 pounds lean ground beef

2 cups peeled, roasted, and diced green chiles

½ cup Mexican red chili powder

2 tablespoons ground cumin

2 cups beef stock (see Basic Stocks on page 25)

Two 28-ounce cans crushed tomatoes, undrained

Two 14-ounce cans pinto beans, drained and rinsed

Salt and freshly ground black pepper

Cook the bacon over medium heat in a large stockpot until crisp (do not discard the bacon fat). Cook the onion and garlic, stirring until translucent, about 5 minutes. Stir in the ground beef and cook for about 5 to 10 minutes, until browned. Fold in the green chiles, red chili powder, cumin, beef stock, and crushed tomatoes.

Cook the chili for another hour. Just prior to serving, mix in the pinto beans and heat through. Season to taste with salt and pepper.

Thai Chicken Chili, Alaskan Style

Makes 4 servings

The influence of Thai and Asian flavors on my cooking shines through in this recipe. The addition of Thai basil and chopped cilantro gives an ordinary chili recipe a Thai twist. It is light enough for summer fare as well as a warming winter dish. Substitute low-sodium chicken broth for a healthy alternative.

¼ cup olive oil

1 medium yellow onion, chopped

2 cloves garlic, minced

2 teaspoons red chile flakes

One 32-ounce can great northern beans, drained and rinsed

1 quart (4 cups) chicken stock (see Basic Stocks on page 25)

1 large tomato, seeded and diced

2 cups shredded cooked chicken meat

Juice of 1 lime (about 2 tablespoons)

1½ teaspoons ground chili powder

1½ teaspoons ground cumin

Kosher salt and freshly ground white pepper

Chopped Thai basil

Chopped cilantro

2 teaspoons freshly grated lime peel

Heat the olive oil in a large stockpot over medium-high heat. Cook the onion, garlic, and chile flakes for about 5 minutes, stirring until tender. Fold in the beans, chicken stock, tomato, chicken, and lime juice. Simmer, uncovered, for about 10 minutes.

Stir in the chili powder and cumin, adjusting to taste. Season with salt and pepper to taste. Just before serving, garnish with basil, cilantro, and lime peel. Serve immediately.

Forest Mushroom Soup
with Kodiak Scallops

Makes 8 servings

This creamy soup is perfectly complemented by adding lightly sautéed Kodiak scallops. It is light enough to serve as a first course, but if you accompany it with some warm bread, it makes for a great informal meal on its own.

½ cup (1 stick) unsalted butter, plus 1 tablespoon

1 cup pureed domestic mushrooms

¼ cup minced celery

¼ cup minced yellow onion

¾ cup all-purpose flour

5 cups chicken stock, warmed (see Basic Stocks on page 25)

½ cup sherry

1 cup half-and-half or heavy cream

1 tablespoon chopped fresh thyme

½ teaspoon ground nutmeg

Kosher salt and freshly ground white pepper

1 to 2 pounds Kodiak scallops (10 to 20), rinsed and patted dry

Melt 1 stick of the butter in a large stockpot over medium heat. Cook and stir the mushrooms, celery, and onion for about 10 minutes, until tender. Add the flour, mixing it into a smooth roux and cooking over low heat until it achieves a slight sheen. Pour in the chicken stock and bring to a boil, stirring vigorously to break up the roux and create a smooth consistency.

Cook the mixture over low heat, stirring often for about 30 to 45 minutes, or until the flour taste is gone. Pour in the sherry and half-and-half. Mix in the thyme and nutmeg and season to taste with salt and pepper. Strain the soup through a fine strainer, pressing down on the vegetables to extract the flavor. Discard solids.

In a medium-size skillet, melt the remaining butter over high heat. Cook the scallops for 2 minutes per side, just to lightly sear them. Garnish each serving of soup with scallops. For additional flavor, drizzle with truffle oil and top with sautéed slices of mushroom.

Midnight Sun Oyster Stew

Makes 4 servings

Alaska is often referred to as the Land of the Midnight Sun. With all those hours of daylight, people up here love to enjoy the outdoors as much as possible. This easy stew makes your kitchen time minimal so you can take full advantage of those long summer days. Whether camping on the beach or enjoying time at home with friends, you'll find that this recipe in its classic simplicity works well anywhere. Garnish with some chopped parsley and oyster crackers.

2 tablespoons unsalted butter

2 tablespoons chopped shallot

2 dozen oysters, shucked with juice reserved (see recipe note on page 6)

3 cups half-and-half

Kosher salt and freshly ground black pepper

Melt the butter in a saucepan over medium-low heat. Cook the shallot for about 1 minute, or until just tender (do not brown). Add the oysters and their reserved juice, tossing to coat. Pour in the half-and-half and bring to a low simmer, cooking uncovered for 2 to 3 minutes.

Season to taste with salt and pepper. Garnish with parsley and oyster crackers before serving.

Ocean Fresh Seafood Gumbo

Makes 8 servings

Practice, practice, practice. Getting the roux right is the only difficult part of this recipe and is the true secret of perfect gumbo. Make sure you read through the recipe carefully before you start, and take your time. Once you have succeeded in the creation of the roux, you will see how important it is to this classic New Orleans dish. Top with minced green onion.

> 1 cup vegetable oil
>
> 1½ cups all-purpose flour
>
> ¾ cup diced green bell pepper
>
> ¾ cup diced yellow onion
>
> ¾ cup diced celery
>
> 1 pound andouille sausage, cut into ¼-inch-thick rounds
>
> 1½ quarts (6 cups) chicken stock, warmed (see Basic Stocks on page 25)
>
> 2 tablespoons olive oil
>
> 1 dozen fresh steamer clams in the shell, rinsed
>
> 1 cup white wine
>
> ½ pound blue mussels, scrubbed and debearded (discard any open mussels)
>
> ½ pound Alaskan scallops, side muscle removed
>
> 1 pound raw Alaskan side stripe or spot shrimp, peeled and deveined
>
> 4 king crab legs, split (about 6 inches long)
>
> Gumbo Seasoning (recipe follows)
>
> 4 cups cooked white rice

In a large cast-iron dutch oven or heavy stockpot, heat the vegetable oil over medium-high heat until it begins to smoke. Mix in the flour and immediately begin stirring (caution: the flour will create steam when it comes in contact with the oil). Stir constantly, scraping the sides and bottom of the pot to ensure that no black spots appear. If black spots appear, the roux is burned and you must start over. Cook until the mixture forms a roux with a smooth texture and achieves a coppery color (like an old penny).

Remove the roux from the heat and stir in the bell pepper, onion, and celery (again, use caution as they will produce a lot of steam). Let the vegetables sit in the roux until they become tender, about 5 minutes. Mix in the sausage and chicken stock and bring the mixture to a full boil. Reduce the heat to a simmer, skimming the foam off as necessary with a spoon. Simmer, uncovered, for about 45 minutes, or until any flour taste is gone.

Meanwhile, in a large sauté pan, heat the olive oil over medium heat until a light haze forms. Add the clams and the white wine. Cover the pan with a tight-fitting lid and cook over high heat. After about 2 minutes, the clams should begin to open. As the first clam opens, add the mussels and replace the lid. Check again after 2 minutes. When it appears that all of the shellfish have opened, add the scallops, shrimp, and crab. Simmer, covered, for about 5 minutes, or until the scallops are just heated through (do not overcook!).

Carefully pour the entire seafood mixture into the dutch oven, gently stirring to combine. Season to taste with the gumbo seasoning, adding a small amount at a time until you reach your desired heat level. Serve over cooked rice and garnish with minced green onion.

Gumbo Seasoning

   1 tablespoon cayenne pepper

   1 tablespoon freshly ground white pepper

   1 tablespoon freshly ground black pepper

   1 tablespoon dried thyme

   1 tablespoon dried basil

In a small bowl, combine the cayenne pepper, white pepper, black pepper, thyme, and basil. Store in an airtight container until ready to use. Can be stored for up to 2 months.

Kincaid Grill's Seafood Fusion

Makes 4 servings

My experience with fusion began when I worked in Hong Kong, Singapore, and Bangkok. This recipe is a personal favorite of mine; I love the fresh aromatic ingredients. It keeps my guests coming back time and time again. Garnish with diced roma tomato, chopped fresh cilantro, and drops of chili oil and basil oil. Note that the starred ingredients are available at most Asian markets.

Two 19-ounce cans coconut milk

1 tablespoon sliced peeled ginger

4 stalks lemongrass*, cut into 1-inch cubes and crushed

8 lime leaves*, torn in half

¼ cup fish sauce*

2 tablespoons granulated sugar

½ tablespoon sambal paste*

Juice of 1 lime (about 2 tablespoons)

½ cup chicken stock, for thinning (see Basic Stocks on page 25)

8 fresh mussels, scrubbed and debearded (discard any open mussels)

3 cups water

Dash salt

12 Shrimp Wontons (recipe follows)

In a large stockpot, combine the coconut milk, ginger, lemongrass, lime leaves, fish sauce, sugar, sambal paste, and lime juice. Bring the mixture to a slow simmer, uncovered, for about 20 minutes. Thin it as needed with the chicken stock. Put the mussels in the stockpot and cook just until they open, about 2 minutes.

In another stockpot, bring the water and salt to a boil. Put the completed wontons in the pot and poach for about 3 minutes.

Divide the wontons among 4 fairly deep serving bowls. Ladle the mussels and broth over the wontons. Serve immediately.

Shrimp Wontons

½ pound raw medium shrimp, peeled and deveined

1 teaspoon minced peeled ginger

1 tablespoon minced green onion (both white and green parts)

1 tablespoon chopped garlic

1 tablespoon fish sauce

1 tablespoon chopped cilantro

1 teaspoon sambal paste

12 wonton wrappers

1 egg, beaten

Put the shrimp, ginger, green onion, garlic, fish sauce, cilantro, and sambal paste in a food processor. Pulse until the mixture is well combined.

Drop about 1 tablespoon of the mixture into each wonton wrapper, folding over and using the egg wash to seal. Place the wontons on a lined baking sheet until ready to use.

Deckhand's Seafood Cioppino

Makes 4 servings

Imagine being on a fishing vessel, out to sea and creating dishes from the day's catch. Cioppino is a lively dish with tons of flavor. The great thing about it is that it can be made from one or fifteen kinds of seafood. This is my take on this San Francisco classic. Serve with crusty French bread.

Cioppino Base

¼ cup olive oil

½ cup diced green bell pepper

½ cup diced celery

½ cup diced yellow onion

½ fennel bulb, scrubbed and cut into 4 to 6 pieces

2 tablespoons minced garlic

1 cup dry white wine

One 28-ounce can crushed plum tomatoes in puree

2 cups clam juice, or fish or chicken stock (see Basic Stocks on page 25)

Kosher salt and freshly ground black pepper

Heat the olive oil in a large stockpot over high heat until smoking. Add the bell pepper, celery, onion, and fennel, cooking and stirring for about 5 minutes, until tender-crisp. Lower the heat slightly and stir in the garlic.

Pour in the wine, deglazing the stockpot by scraping up any browned bits on the bottom. Stir with a wooden spoon until the wine is almost evaporated, then mix in the tomatoes and clam juice. The consistency should be rather thin, just coating the back of the spoon.

Season with salt and pepper to taste and remove from the heat. The cioppino base can be prepared up to 2 days in advance and refrigerated in an airtight container until needed.

Seafood

2 tablespoons olive oil

1 dozen fresh steamer clams in the shell, rinsed (discard any open clams)

1 cup white wine

½ pound blue mussels, scrubbed and debearded (discard any open mussels)

4 medium red potatoes, parboiled and quartered

½ pound sea scallops, side muscle removed

1 pound raw Alaskan spot shrimp, peeled and deveined

4 king crab legs, split

2 tablespoons chopped fresh herbs (equal parts tarragon, thyme, oregano, and basil)

2 tablespoons chopped fresh parsley

In a 4-quart saucepan, heat the olive oil over medium heat until just smoking. Add the clams and wine. Cover with a tight-fitting lid and cook over high heat for about 2 minutes, or until the clams begin to open. As the first clams begin to open, add the mussels and potatoes. Cover again and cook for another 2 minutes, or until the mussels have all started to open.

Stir in the cioppino base and add the scallops, shrimp, and crab legs. Simmer the seafood mixture, covered, until just heated through, about 5 minutes. Be careful not to overcook the seafood.

Stir in the herbs and garnish with parsley. Serve immediately.

Cream of Butternut Squash Soup

Makes 6 to 8 servings

Those of you who garden know that if you plant squash, it will come. You're likely to end up with an overabundance that you have difficulty pawning off on anyone, even friends and family. This recipe makes use of the mild flavor of butternut squash, creating a soup that is a perfect beginning to a holiday meal or other special occasion. Experiment with other varieties of squash to see what you can create! This soup is also wonderful with garnishes of toasted hazelnuts, pan-roasted apples or pears, or crisp bits of bacon. Add the garnishes to each individual bowl just before serving.

½ cup (1 stick) unsalted butter

1 cup pureed roasted butternut squash

¼ cup minced yellow onion

¼ cup minced celery

¾ cup all-purpose flour

6 cups chicken stock, heated (see Basic Stocks on page 25)

1 cup half-and-half

1 tablespoon fresh thyme leaves

½ teaspoon ground nutmeg

Kosher salt and freshly ground white pepper to taste

In a heavy 4-quart stockpot, heat the butter over medium heat. Add the squash, onion, and celery and sweat the mixture (cover and cook over medium heat) for about 5 to 7 minutes, or until tender. Add the flour, mixing until it forms a roux. Cook the roux over low heat until it develops a sheen, about 3 to 4 minutes. Add the chicken stock, bringing to a light boil and stirring constantly to break up the roux and form a smooth consistency.

Reduce the heat to low and cook for about 30 to 45 minutes or until the flour taste is gone. Add the half-and-half, thyme, and nutmeg and stir well. Run the soup through a strainer, pressing the vegetables against the mesh of the strainer to remove all of the flavor. Discard solids. Add salt and pepper to taste. Return the soup to low heat until ready to serve.

Thai-Style Cabbage Wraps

Makes 4 to 6 servings

These little salad cups can be served as an appetizer or as your salad course. They are meant to be eaten by hand, using the cabbage leaves as you would a tortilla or taco shell. Top with chopped fresh cilantro and a few mint sprigs.

¼ cup uncooked jasmine rice

¼ cup fish sauce

Juice of 2 limes (about ¼ cup)

1 pound cooked and shredded chicken

Ground Thai red chile powder, or flakes

¼ cup minced red onion

¼ cup minced green onion (both white and green parts)

2 tablespoons chopped fresh mint

3 tablespoons chopped fresh cilantro

1 head napa cabbage

Toast the jasmine rice in a small pan over medium-high heat, tossing constantly until it is evenly browned. Remove the rice from the pan immediately to keep it from burning. Let it cool, then pulse the rice in a coffee grinder until coarsely ground (be careful not to overgrind the rice).

In a medium bowl, combine the fish sauce and lime juice; let the chicken marinate in the mixture for 10 minutes in the refrigerator.

Heat a sauté pan over medium heat and cook the chicken with the marinade until heated through, about 5 minutes. Remove the chicken from the heat and let cool.

Season the chicken to taste with red chile powder. Stir in the red onion, green onion, mint, and cilantro. Dust the mixture with the toasted ground rice to absorb any excess liquid. Be sure not to make it too dry; you should have some moisture left.

Spoon the chicken salad onto a serving platter, arranging whole cabbage leaves around the platter. To serve, spoon the mixture into a cabbage leaf and eat by hand.

Traditional Caesar Salad

Makes 8 servings

After working in several different establishments, I've learned that every chef has their favorite Caesar salad recipe. This is the one I've created and made my own. You'll find that the simplicity of the croutons does not overpower the dressing in the salad. Great as a starter for steaks or other dishes, it can also be served as main fare topped with fish or chicken. For an interesting twist, make it a minted Caesar by adding 2 tablespoons of chopped fresh mint and ½ cup of crisp-cooked, crumbled bacon. Top with hand-shaved Parmesan.

3 egg yolks

1 tablespoon anchovy paste

1 tablespoon Dijon mustard

3 cloves garlic, chopped

⅓ cup red wine vinegar

Juice of 1 lemon (about 3 tablespoons)

2 tablespoons Worcestershire sauce

1 cup grated Parmesan cheese (about 8 ounces)

1½ cups olive oil

Salt and freshly ground black pepper

2 heads romaine lettuce, washed, dried, and torn into bite-size pieces

1 to 2 cups Croutons (recipe follows)

In a blender, combine the egg yolks, anchovy paste, mustard, garlic, red wine vinegar, lemon juice, and Worcestershire sauce. While the blender is on, slowly add the Parmesan and drizzle in the olive oil to emulsify. Season with salt and pepper to taste.

Put the romaine in a large salad bowl and toss with the dressing. Add the croutons and shaved Parmesan on top. Serve immediately.

Croutons

1 loaf French bread (preferably stale or day old)

½ cup olive oil

Preheat the oven to 400°F.

Cut the bread into 1-inch cubes. In a large bowl, toss the bread cubes to coat with the olive oil. Spread the bread cubes on a baking sheet.

Place the baking sheet in the middle of the oven and bake until golden brown, about 5 to 7 minutes. Remove and allow the croutons to crisp at room temperature. Use immediately or store in a tightly covered container for up to 1 week.

Poached Pear Salad
with Fireweed Honey–Pepper Vinaigrette

Makes 4 servings

Another staple of Kincaid Grill, this summer salad has a sweet and nutty flavor. The spicy honey dressing coupled with the Gorgonzola and crunchy pecans makes for the ultimate in textures and flavors. You can, of course, use any kind of honey, but the bite of Alaska's fireweed honey does add some extra zest to this salad.

2 Poached Pears (recipe follows)

¼ cup crumbled Gorgonzola cheese

¼ cup Candied Pecans (recipe follows)

1 bunch mixed greens, rinsed and patted dry

Fireweed Honey–Pepper Vinaigrette (recipe follows)

Freshly ground black pepper

Assemble the salad by combining the pears, cheese, candied pecans, and mixed greens in a large bowl. Then lightly toss with the vinaigrette. Season to taste with pepper.

Poached Pears

2 cups red table wine

¼ cup red wine vinegar

2 cinnamon sticks

2 tablespoons fresh lemon juice

1 bay leaf

2 pears, any variety, cored, peeled, and halved

Water for covering

Put the wine, vinegar, cinnamon sticks, lemon juice, and bay leaf in a medium saucepan. Bring the mixture to a simmer over medium heat.

Put the pears in the liquid, adding enough water to cover them. Use a plate or small lid to hold the pears down in the water while poaching. Poach for 30 minutes, or until a knife inserted in the center goes in easily.

Remove the saucepan from the heat and cool. The pears and the poaching liquid can be stored in the refrigerator for up to 3 days. Serve chilled.

Candied Pecans

Canola oil, 2 inches deep in fryer

1 cup confectioners' sugar

½ teaspoon cayenne pepper

½ teaspoon salt

2 cups boiling water

1 cup pecan halves

Heat the canola oil in a deep-fryer to about 350°F.

Meanwhile, combine the sugar, cayenne pepper, and salt in a small bowl and set aside. In a medium-size saucepan, boil the water. Drop the pecans in the boiling water, then pour them through a strainer after about 5 seconds. Pour the sugar-pepper-salt mixture over the pecans, tossing to coat. Spread the pecans over a baking sheet to separate.

Carefully drop the coated pecans in the deep-fryer, cooking until they stop fizzing, about 1 minute. Do not overfry or they will become bitter. Spread the pecans out on parchment paper and allow them to crisp at room temperature.

Fireweed Honey-Pepper Vinaigrette

½ cup fireweed honey (any honey will do)

1 tablespoon Tabasco sauce

⅓ cup rice wine vinegar

¼ teaspoon salt

¼ teaspoon freshly ground black pepper

½ cup vegetable oil

½ cup walnut oil

In a blender, combine the honey, Tabasco sauce, vinegar, salt, and pepper. With the blender running, slowly add the vegetable oil and the walnut oil, one at a time, to emulsify. Use immediately or store in the refrigerator in an airtight container for up to 2 weeks.

From-the-Sea Shellfish Salad

Makes 4 servings

This fusion-style salad combines only the freshest Alaskan seafood. You can substitute or leave out according to your personal preference, as this is a very versatile recipe. The amount of curry paste in the dressing will dictate the spice, so if you like to turn up the heat, add a little more curry. Top with black sesame seeds and green onions cut on the diagonal.

> 1 dozen fresh mussels, scrubbed and debearded (discard any open mussels)
>
> 1 dozen fresh clams in the shell, rinsed (discard any open clams)
>
> ¾ cup white wine
>
> 1 tablespoon chopped garlic
>
> 4 Alaskan oysters (optional), shucked (see recipe note on page 6)
>
> 8 cooked snow crab claws (may be found at your local fish market; ask to have the shells cut to expose the meat)
>
> 12 Chinese pea pods
>
> ½ cup flower-cut carrots
>
> ½ cup julienne red onion
>
> ½ cup chopped celery
>
> 4 radishes, cut into ¼-inch-thick slices
>
> ½ medium red bell pepper, julienne
>
> ½ to ¾ cup (about 4 to 6 ounces) Red Chile Lime Dressing (recipe follows)
>
> 1 bunch mixed greens, rinsed and patted dry

Put the mussels and clams in a large stockpot with the wine and garlic. Cover and cook over medium heat, steaming until the shellfish open (note that the mussels will be done far ahead of the clams). After the shells have opened, remove them from the stockpot, cover with plastic wrap, and put in the refrigerator until cool.

Take the liquid from the stockpot and reduce by half, then pour the reserved liquid into a small bowl to cool to room temperature.

Arrange the oysters, snow crab claws, mussels, and clams along the edges of a large serving platter. Put the pea pods, carrot, red onion, celery, radishes, and red pepper in a bowl. Mix in the greens. Toss the vegetables with half the dressing. Place the vegetable-greens mixture in the middle of the serving platter.

Drizzle the remaining dressing over the shellfish. Garnish with green onions and black sesame seeds.

Red Chile Lime Dressing

¼ cup shellfish stock (from reserve)

Juice of 4 limes (about ½ cup)

1 tablespoon minced peeled ginger

2 tablespoons fish sauce

1 teaspoon red curry paste

1 tablespoon chopped garlic

¼ cup olive oil

2 tablespoons chopped fresh mint

2 tablespoons chopped fresh cilantro

Salt and freshly ground black pepper

In a blender, combine the shellfish stock, lime juice, ginger, fish sauce, curry paste, and garlic. With the blender on, slowly drizzle in the olive oil to emulsify. Mix in the mint and cilantro.

Season with salt and pepper to taste. Use the dressing immediately or refrigerate in an airtight container until needed, or up to 1 week.

Kincaid Grill's Scallop Niçoise

Makes 6 servings

The word niçoise loosely translates to "in the style of Nice, France," which is where this recipe originated long ago. I've given it a bit of an Alaskan twist by substituting the traditional tuna with fresh scallops. Drizzle with extra virgin olive oil and garnish with chopped fresh parsley. This salad is a guest favorite at Kincaid Grill.

1 pound red potatoes, blanched and cut into ¼-inch-thick slices

½ pound fresh green beans, blanched

3 eggs, hard-boiled and chopped

½ cup Mustard Vinaigrette (recipe follows)

½ cup Olive Tapenade (recipe follows)

1 pound Alaskan sea scallops, rinsed and patted dry

Pinch kosher salt and freshly ground pepper

¼ cup extra virgin olive oil

Prepare the red potatoes, green beans, eggs, olive tapenade, and mustard vinaigrette, and store each item in the refrigerator until needed.

Put the scallops, salt, pepper, and olive oil in a glass dish to marinate in the refrigerator for 10 minutes.

Heat a gas or charcoal grill to medium high. Discard the marinade and grill the scallops for about 2 minutes per side, until medium rare, or sear them quickly in a sauté pan with a bit more olive oil. Scallops are done when they spring back lightly to the touch.

Gently toss the red potatoes, green beans, and hard-boiled eggs with the mustard vinaigrette in a medium-size bowl. Divide the mixture evenly onto 6 serving plates. Place the scallops and a dollop of olive tapenade on top. Drizzle with extra virgin olive oil and garnish with parsley. Serve immediately.

Mustard Vinaigrette

1 tablespoon stone-ground mustard

½ shallot, finely chopped (about 2 tablespoons)

1 teaspoon minced garlic

½ cup red wine vinegar

1½ cups extra virgin olive oil

Kosher salt and freshly ground black pepper

In a blender, combine the mustard, shallot, garlic, and vinegar. Running the blender slowly, drizzle in the olive oil. Season with salt and pepper to taste. Use immediately or store the vinaigrette in the refrigerator for up to 1 week.

Olive Tapenade

8 ounces Greek olives, pitted

1 ounce anchovy fillets, soaked in cold water to remove the salt

1 clove garlic, minced

2 tablespoons capers

2 tablespoons stone-ground mustard

2 teaspoons chopped fresh parsley

¼ cup extra virgin olive oil

Kosher salt and freshly ground black pepper

In a food processor, combine the olives, anchovies, garlic, capers, mustard, and parsley. Work in a little of the olive oil at a time until well combined. The tapenade should appear somewhat rustic, with bits of olive and caper visible.

Season with salt and pepper to taste. Use immediately or refrigerate until needed, up to 1 week.

Grilled Spot Shrimp Salad

Makes 4 servings

This salad can work well as a main meal on those long summer days when no one feels much like cooking. It is quick and easy, and can be prepared in advance and assembled right before dinner. Garnish with chopped fresh basil.

¼ cup olive oil

2 tablespoons minced garlic

2 tablespoons chopped fresh herbs (equal parts basil, parsley, thyme, and oregano)

Salt and freshly ground black pepper

2 pounds raw Alaskan spot shrimp (about 32), peeled and deveined

Tomato Feta Mix (recipe follows)

½ cup reduced balsamic vinegar (see recipe note below)

To prepare a balsamic vinegar reduction: In a small saucepan, heat 1 cup of balsamic vinegar and 1 tablespoon of sugar on medium heat until it is reduced by half, being careful not to scorch the mixture. Chill in the refrigerator until cooled and the consistency of a light syrup.

In a glass baking dish, combine the olive oil, garlic, and herbs. Season with salt and pepper to taste. Put in the shrimp and marinate in the refrigerator for up to 2 hours.

Heat a gas or charcoal grill on high. Discard the marinade and cook the shrimp until just done, so they are pink but not too firm. Put the shrimp in the refrigerator to cool.

Divide the shrimp evenly among 4 serving plates. Put a dollop of the tomato feta mix in the center of each plate. Garnish with fresh basil and drizzle with the balsamic vinegar reduction.

Tomato Feta Mix

1 cup diced ripe tomato

¼ cup crumbled feta cheese

¼ cup oil-cured or kalamata olives

3 tablespoons chopped fresh basil

3 tablespoons olive oil

1 tablespoon red wine vinegar

2 teaspoons minced garlic

2 teaspoons fresh lemon juice

Salt and freshly ground black pepper

In a medium-size bowl, combine the tomato, feta cheese, olives, basil, olive oil, vinegar, garlic, and lemon juice. Season with salt and pepper to taste. Store in the refrigerator for up to 2 days in an airtight container until ready to use.

Poached Alaskan Salmon Salad with Mustard Vinaigrette

Makes 4 servings

Salmon is a staple here in Alaska, and sometimes we get tired of the same old recipes. This is a nice, light salad that provides something new for those salmon fillets in your freezer. Poaching fish gives it a very light and moist flavor. Salmon is especially nice prepared this way, and the mustard vinaigrette rounds out the flavor quite well. Garnish with sprigs of tarragon for an elegant presentation.

3 cups water

2 cups dry white wine

2 to 4 sprigs tarragon, leaves removed and coarsely chopped (reserve the stems)

2 bay leaves

1 teaspoon whole black peppercorns

1 lemon, cut into ¼-inch-thick slices

4 salmon fillets (about 6 ounces each), skinned and boned

¼ cup Dijon mustard

3 tablespoons white wine vinegar

¾ cup plus 1 tablespoon olive oil

⅔ cup chopped shallot

Salt and freshly ground black pepper

2 bunches mixed greens, rinsed and patted dry

In large pot or skillet, combine the water and wine. Add the tarragon stems, bay leaves, peppercorns, and lemon. Bring the mixture to a boil and cook for 15 to 20 minutes. Reduce to a simmer and add the salmon fillets. Cover and simmer for another 10 to 12 minutes.

Turn off the heat and allow the salmon to cool in the pan. When the salmon is completely cold, remove the fillets and drain them on paper towels. Cover the fillets with plastic wrap and refrigerate for 1 to 2 hours, or until ready to serve.

To prepare the mustard vinaigrette, combine the mustard and vinegar in a small bowl. Gradually whisk in ¾ cup of the olive oil. Stir in the shallot and tarragon leaves. Season with salt and pepper to taste and set aside.

In a large bowl, toss the mixed greens with the remaining 1 tablespoon of olive oil. Season with salt and pepper to taste. Arrange the greens on 4 plates. Top each with a piece of the salmon. Spoon some of the mustard vinaigrette over the fish until it is coated. Garnish with more sprigs of tarragon.

Pioneer Peak Potato Pancake Salad
with Smoked Salmon
and White Truffle Vinaigrette

Makes 4 servings

Growing up loving my mom's potato pancakes (which we ate with strawberry jam), I thought it fitting that I find a recipe that combines the great taste of these classic pancakes with some of my favorites—watercress and smoked salmon. The white truffle vinaigrette adds a rich elegance to the recipe. I am partial to fresh Alaskan "Pioneer" potatoes from the valley, but of course any potato works just fine. Top the potato pancakes with a dollop of sour cream and some minced chives.

2 cups grated parbaked potatoes (still firm, chilled)

2 eggs, whisked

¼ cup minced yellow onion

1 to 2 tablespoons all-purpose flour

1 to 2 tablespoons milk

Salt and freshly ground black pepper

1 tablespoon olive oil

8 ounces smoked salmon, flaked and warmed

1 bunch watercress

White Truffle Vinaigrette (recipe follows)

In a large bowl, combine the potatoes, eggs, and onion. Stir in the flour to form a paste and enough milk to make it smooth and batterlike. Season with salt and pepper to taste.

Heat the olive oil on a flat griddle on medium heat. For each pancake, spoon ¼ cup of the mixture onto the griddle, flattening slightly with a spatula. Cook for about 4 minutes on each side, until the potato pancakes are well browned. Set them aside on a warm platter for later use. The pancakes can also be prepared up to 1 day ahead and reheated.

In a medium-sized bowl, gently mix together the salmon, watercress, and 2 tablespoons of the vinaigrette. Arrange the mixture along the perimeter of a large serving platter. Put the pancakes in the center of the platter. Dollop with sour cream and garnish with chives. Drizzle the remaining vinaigrette over the platter.

White Truffle Vinaigrette

1 tablespoon minced shallot

¼ cup white wine vinegar

Salt and freshly ground black pepper

¾ cup vegetable oil

2 teaspoons white truffle oil (available at specialty shops or the gourmet section of most grocery stores)

In a blender, pulse together the shallot and vinegar. Season with salt and pepper to taste. With the blender running, slowly drizzle in the vegetable oil and the white truffle oil to emulsify.

Seafood

Fresh and Spicy Mussels in White Wine

Kodiak Island Scallop Crepes with Wild Mushrooms and Herbs

Scallop Mousse with Pine Nut Crust and Pesto Cream

Roast Salmon with Mat-Su Summer Corn Relish

Seared Copper River Salmon with Leeks and Wild Mushroom Ragout

Alaskan King Salmon with Arugula Pesto

Ginger-Peppered Silver Salmon

Denali Summit Soy Salmon with Cilantro Coconut Chutney

Kenai Special Salmon with Prosciutto and Saffron Tomato Salsa

Prosciutto Apple Salmon with Honey Mustard Vinaigrette

Wildfire Smoked Salmon Hash

Pan-Seared Salmon with Horseradish Parmesan Crust

Pistachio-Roasted Resurrection Bay Halibut with
Sweet and Sour Swiss Chard

Seward's Bounty Halibut Piccata

Peppered Halibut with Ginger Butter

Locals-Only Halibut Olympia

Hawaiian Halibut, Alaskan Style

Halibut Amandine

Summer Sea Bass with Saffron Tomato Sauce

Fish, to taste right, must swim
three times—in water, in butter, in wine.
—Polish proverb

WHEN I FIRST MOVED TO ALASKA, I worked at the Crow's Nest Restaurant at the Hotel Captain Cook. One day the entire kitchen crew decided to go fishing at Alexander Creek on our day off. We planned our trip carefully, full of excitement about the hordes of fish we were going to catch. As the entire kitchen staff was going, we had just one full day to fish and camp, since the restaurant was closed only on Mondays. We made it to our spot and fished all day on Monday. We got . . . nothing. Not one tiny fish graced our lines. We didn't even see them swimming around taunting us!

We were all very disappointed, and after drowning our sorrows over the campfire that night, went to bed and resigned ourselves to going home empty-handed. Early Tuesday morning, we woke to an odd splashing sound coming from the creek outside our tents. We got to up to investigate. It seemed that overnight the Silver run had arrived! Fish were everywhere, all fighting to be the first to hit our lines. We quickly limited out and were able to head home with our coolers full of fresh fish. It just goes to show you that sometimes a day can make all the difference and to never give up the dream too soon.

All fish stories aside (don't get me started on the one that got away), the abundance of seafood in Alaska is legendary and a huge part of our local culture. Using fresh seafood can make a huge difference in the end result of your meal.

When selecting seafood, make sure it has an ocean smell, as opposed to a "fishy" aroma, and that the eyes and scales of your fish are clear, with firm flesh.

Fresh and Spicy Mussels in White Wine

Makes 4 to 6 servings

Mussels are always best when fresh and lightly cooked. It is important to make sure they open when cooking and to discard any that do not open. This dish works as either an appetizer or main fare.

⅓ cup olive oil

½ medium yellow onion, cut into ¼-inch-thick slices

4 cloves garlic, chopped

2 tablespoons grated fennel bulb

1 teaspoon dried crushed red pepper

½ teaspoon salt

1 cup dry white wine

2 lemon slices, ¼ inch thick

½ cup chopped fresh parsley

2½ pounds fresh mussels, scrubbed and debearded

Freshly ground black pepper

½ cup chopped seeded tomatoes

Heat the olive oil in a large stockpot over medium-high heat. Stir in the onion, garlic, fennel, red pepper, and salt. Cook the mixture until the onion is light brown, about 4 minutes. Add the wine, lemon slices, and ¼ cup of the parsley, bringing it all to a boil.

Carefully put the mussels into the stockpot. Cover and cook until the mussels open (stirring once to rearrange the mussels), about 6 minutes. Discard any mussels that do not open.

Using a slotted spoon, transfer the mussels to a large shallow bowl. Continue to boil the broth in the stockpot until it reduces to 1 cup, about 3 minutes. Season to taste with pepper. Pour the broth over the mussels. Sprinkle with the tomatoes and remaining parsley. Serve immediately.

Kodiak Island Scallop Crepes with Wild Mushrooms and Herbs

Makes 4 to 6 servings

The French style of crepes combined with Alaska's own Kodiak scallops makes for an elegant dinner or brunch item. Garnish with a bit of fresh parsley and serve with a green salad. Experiment with this recipe, as the crepes work well with any savory filling. The crepes can even be used in lieu of bread.

Crepe Batter

> 1 tablespoon butter (or nonstick coating)
>
> 2 cups milk
>
> 2 eggs, beaten
>
> 1 cup all-purpose flour
>
> 1 tablespoon chopped fresh herbs (equal parts thyme, basil, and parsley)
>
> 1 tablespoon minced chives
>
> Salt and freshly ground black pepper

Melt the butter in a small nonstick skillet over medium heat. In a mixing bowl, beat together the milk and eggs. Fold in the flour, herbs, and chives. Season with salt and pepper to taste.

Using a 1-ounce (⅛ cup) ladle, spoon a ladleful of batter into the skillet, tilting so the batter spreads thinly over the pan's surface. Cook until light brown, about 1 minute, flipping the crepe over with a small spatula (or fingers if you are brave!) to cook the other side.

Remove the crepe to a warm platter and repeat the steps until all of the batter is used.

Scallop Mixture

> 2 tablespoons olive oil
>
> 1 pound Alaskan sea scallops, rinsed and patted dry

Salt and freshly ground black pepper

4 ounces mixed specialty mushrooms, chopped

2 tablespoons chopped shallot

1 tablespoon chopped fresh herbs (equal parts thyme, basil, and parsley)

1 tablespoon chopped garlic

¼ cup sherry

1 cup basic white sauce (see recipe note below)

To prepare a basic white sauce: In a small, heavy-bottomed saucepan, melt ¼ cup (½ stick) unsalted butter over medium heat. Whisk in ¼ cup all-purpose flour. Cook over medium heat for 3 minutes. Add 2 cups whole milk and a pinch of ground nutmeg and whisk vigorously until thickened, about 5 minutes. Lower the heat and cook for an additional 45 minutes, until the flour taste is gone. Season with salt and white pepper to taste. Strain through a fine strainer to remove any lumps. The sauce can be stored in the refrigerator for up to 1 week.

Heat the olive oil in a small skillet over medium heat. Season the scallops with salt and pepper, and cook to medium-rare, about 2 minutes per side. Remove the scallops and store on a warm platter.

Add more oil to the skillet if necessary. Cook and stir the mushrooms with the shallot, herbs, and garlic. Deglaze with the sherry, scraping up any browned bits from the bottom of the skillet.

In a small saucepan, prepare a basic white sauce (see the recipe note above). Add the white sauce to the mushroom-shallot-herb-garlic mixture and heat through. Season to taste with salt and pepper. Slice the scallops and add to the mixture, then remove from heat.

Spoon a small amount of the mixture into each crepe and roll into a tube shape. Drizzle with any remaining white sauce if you like and serve immediately.

Scallop Mousse with Pine Nut Crust and Pesto Cream

Makes 4 servings

Although this recipe looks very impressive and intimidating, it is surprisingly easy to make. Chef Kevin of AVTEC (Alaska Vocational Technical College in Seward) originally gave me the idea for this, as it is a variation of a recipe he used at a Seward family gathering. My wife's aunt Carol Ann loved the dish and insisted that I figure out how to make it too. With my own modifications to Kevin's original recipe, it has become a popular part of my repertoire. Garnish with fried basil leaves (see the recipe note below), lemon slices, and roasted red peppers.

> **1 cup heavy cream**
>
> **¼ cup basil pesto sauce (homemade or store-bought; see recipe note below)**
>
> **Salt and freshly ground black pepper**
>
> **¾ pound Alaskan sea scallops, rinsed and patted dry**
>
> **½ teaspoon salt**
>
> **½ cup toasted pine nuts, coarsely chopped**

To make basil pesto sauce: In a food processor fitted with a metal blade, combine 1 cup fresh basil leaves, 1 teaspoon chopped garlic, 2 tablespoons freshly grated Parmesan, 1 tablespoon toasted pine nuts, ½ cup olive oil, and salt and pepper to taste. Process until pureed.

To prepare fried basil leaves: In a sauté pan, heat 2 tablespoons of vegetable oil over medium heat. Place fresh basil leaves in the oil and fry until translucent, about 30 seconds, turning once. Drain on a paper towel. Use caution when cooking, as basil leaves tend to pop in the oil due to their moisture content.

Pour ½ cup of the heavy cream into a medium-size saucepan, reserving the remainder in the refrigerator. Reduce the cream until it begins to thicken and then whisk in the basil pesto sauce. Season with salt and pepper to taste, set aside, and keep warm.

Remove any of the tough bit of muscle on the side of the scallops, if necessary. Puree the scallops and the salt in a food processor until well blended. With the motor running, slowly pour in the remaining cream. Blend until smooth.

Form the scallop mixture into a shape using ring mold or a scoop. Once the mousse is formed, remove the mold and coat the top and bottom with the pine nuts.

Carefully cook over medium-low heat, until the mousse is just heated through. Spoon the sauce onto a warm plate and place the mousse in the center. Garnish as desired and serve immediately.

Roast Salmon
with Mat-Su Summer Corn Relish

Makes 4 to 6 servings

Feel free to cook this salmon up on the grill as opposed to roasting if you prefer. This is a light and healthy meal and will be enjoyed by all. Salmon is high in omega-3 oils, which makes this recipe a heart-healthy and low-fat meal, without sacrificing taste.

> **2½ tablespoons whole coriander seeds**
>
> **¼ cup olive oil**
>
> **Juice of 2 lemons (about ¼ cup)**
>
> **2 tablespoons honey**
>
> **2 tablespoons paprika**
>
> **2 teaspoons salt**
>
> **4 to 6 salmon fillets (about 5 to 6 ounces each)**
>
> **Mat-Su Summer Corn Relish (recipe follows)**

Preheat the oven to 400°F.

In a small skillet, toast the coriander seeds over medium heat for about 1 minute, until they become aromatic. Remove from the heat and cool slightly. Crush the seeds with a pestle or a large flat spoon and set aside.

Line a baking sheet with foil.

Combine the olive oil, lemon juice, honey, paprika, and salt in a bowl. Stir in about half the toasted coriander seeds, reserving the remainder for the relish. Brush the mixture over both sides of the salmon fillets until they are well coated. Transfer the salmon to the baking sheet and cook to the desired doneness, about 10 to 15 minutes.

Place the cooked salmon on a large serving platter and top with corn relish, serving immediately.

Mat-Su Summer Corn Relish

2 medium red bell peppers, whole

2 tablespoons olive oil

2 cups fresh corn kernels (about 2 to 3 ears' worth)

2 green onions, finely chopped (both white and green parts)

2 cloves garlic, minced

1 tablespoon chopped fresh thyme

1 ounce dry white wine

1 tablespoon fresh lemon juice

½ tablespoon honey

2 tablespoons chopped fresh Italian parsley

Salt and freshly ground black pepper

Char the red bell peppers over an open flame until they are blackened. Put them in a sealed plastic bag for about 10 minutes to help release the peel. Peel and seed the peppers, and cut into ½-inch slices. Set aside.

Heat 1 tablespoon of the olive oil in a large skillet over medium-high heat. Mix in the corn and the green onions. Cook and stir the mixture until the corn begins to brown a bit, about 5 minutes. Add the garlic and thyme, continuing to stir for about 2 minutes more. Pour in the wine and cook and stir until the liquid evaporates, then remove from the heat.

Stir in the red bell peppers, lemon juice, honey, and remaining olive oil. Mix in the remaining crushed coriander seeds (from the salmon recipe on the previous page). Throw in the parsley and season with salt and pepper to taste.

This can be made up to 8 hours in advance. Store, covered, in the refrigerator and reheat when ready to use.

Seared Copper River Salmon with Leeks
and Wild Mushroom Ragout

Makes 4 servings

Salmon is a very versatile fish. Its distinct flavor complements almost any ingredients. This is a favorite recipe of mine, not too complicated but with an excellent presentation. It goes very well with my Truffle Potatoes (see page 156). The mushroom ragout could also work as a side dish for steaks or other meats.

4 leeks, rinsed and split

6 tablespoons clarified unsalted butter (see recipe note on page 34)

½ cup chicken stock (see Basic Stocks on page 25)

Salt and freshly ground black pepper

1 salmon fillet (about 2 pounds)

1 cup Wild Mushroom Ragout (recipe follows)

1 cup Pinot Noir Sauce (recipe follows)

Cut the very tip and green tail off of the leeks, and wash and dry thoroughly. Place them cut sides down in a medium-size skillet and sear over medium-high heat with 2 tablespoons of the clarified butter until lightly browned. Turn and sear the other sides. Pour in the chicken stock, and season with salt and pepper to taste. Simmer the mixture, covered, until tender, about 20 minutes. Set aside.

Preheat the oven to 400°F.

In a large skillet, heat the remaining clarified butter until smoking. Place the salmon fillets skin side up and sear until a light crust forms. Turn and sear the other side. Put the salmon with the leeks and mushroom ragout on a baking sheet. Cook for 8 to 10 minutes, or until heated through.

Place the leeks and the ragout on a serving platter, with the salmon fillets on top. Drizzle with the pinot noir sauce and serve immediately.

Wild Mushroom Ragout

2 tablespoons extra virgin olive oil

¼ cup julienne leeks

2 tablespoons chopped shallot

8 ounces fresh mixed specialty mushrooms (any varieties)

¼ cup chopped sun-dried tomatoes

2 tablespoons white wine

1 tablespoon chopped fresh herbs (equal parts thyme, basil, parsley, and oregano)

Salt and freshly ground black pepper

Heat the olive oil in a skillet over medium heat. Cook and stir the leeks and shallots until they are tender, about 5 minutes. Add the mushrooms, continuing to cook and stir until just heated through. Stir in the tomatoes and deglaze with the wine, scraping up any browned bits from the bottom of the skillet.

Mix in the herbs and season to taste with salt and pepper.

Pinot Noir Sauce

1 cup pinot noir

1 cup veal stock (see Basic Stocks on page 25)

In a saucepan over medium heat, reduce the wine by half, stirring often. Pour in the veal stock and reduce again by half.

For a very quick version of this sauce, substitute a brown gravy mix for the veal stock. Do not reduce a second time; just stir until thoroughly combined and the sauce is heated through.

Alaskan King Salmon
with Arugula Pesto

Makes 4 servings

Using parchment paper to cook fish seals in the moisture and makes it extremely flavorful. It is also a very easy yet showy presentation and involves minimal cleanup, a bonus for any host! I love this dish because of its clean simplicity and purity of flavor.

½ cup julienne leeks

½ cup julienne carrots

½ cup julienne celery

½ cup peeled, seeded, and diced tomatoes (or one 15-ounce can diced tomatoes)

4 salmon fillets (about 6 ounces each)

Kosher salt and freshly ground black pepper

4 teaspoons white wine

1 egg white

Arugula Pesto (recipe follows)

Preheat the oven to 350°F.

Cut 4 pieces of parchment paper into large heart shapes, making sure you leave enough room to fold it over. Combine the leeks, carrots, celery, and tomatoes in a bowl, then place a small amount of the mixture onto each piece of paper, reserving half of the mixture for the next step.

Season the salmon fillets with salt and pepper to taste and place them on top of the vegetable mixture. Cover the salmon fillets with the remaining vegetable mixture and drizzle with wine. Brush the egg white along the edges of the parchment paper to help seal. Fold over the paper and crimp the edges until a package is formed.

Carefully put the parchment packages on a baking sheet and cook in the oven for 15 to 18 minutes, or until the paper is puffed out. Cut open the packages and drizzle with the pesto. Serve immediately.

Arugula Pesto

  1 cup arugula, rinsed well and patted dry

  1 teaspoon chopped garlic

  ½ cup olive oil

  ¼ cup grated Parmesan cheese (2 ounces)

  ¼ cup toasted pine nuts

  Salt and freshly ground black pepper

Combine the arugula, garlic, olive oil, Parmesan, and pine nuts in a food processor and blend until smooth. Adjust the amount of olive oil as necessary for your desired consistency. Season with salt and pepper to taste. Store in an airtight container in the refrigerator until ready to use.

Ginger-Peppered Silver Salmon

Makes 4 servings

Fresh ginger really brings out the flavor of Alaskan salmon. Enjoy this with a nice summer salad. You can also substitute halibut; I've made it with both and had equally great results. Chef's hint: Prepare the vinaigrette on the day of service so the cilantro doesn't discolor. Garnish this dish with black sesame seeds, fresh cilantro, or crisp fried wonton strips (cut some wonton wrappers into thin slices and fry in a bit of canola oil until golden brown).

> **2 tablespoons olive oil**
>
> **2 tablespoons grated peeled ginger**
>
> **2 tablespoons freshly ground black pepper**
>
> **Salt**
>
> **4 salmon fillets (about 6 ounces each)**
>
> **1 cup julienne mixed vegetables (your choice)**
>
> **2 cups cooked white rice, warm and ready to serve**
>
> **Ginger Vinaigrette (recipe follows)**

Heat the olive oil in a large, nonstick skillet over medium-high heat.

In a small bowl, combine the ginger and pepper. Rub each salmon fillet with the ginger-pepper mixture, and season with salt to taste. Sear the salmon skin side up until a nice crust forms. Turn the fillets and repeat the process, cooking until just heated through (do not overcook!). Remove the salmon from the skillet and reserve on a warm platter. Cook the vegetables in the same skillet until heated but still crisp.

Place a scoop of white rice in the center of each serving plate, topping with the vegetables and salmon. Drizzle the entire dish with vinaigrette. Garnish as desired and serve immediately.

Ginger Vinaigrette

1 tablespoon minced peeled ginger

2 tablespoons chopped shallot

2 tablespoons rice vinegar

1 tablespoon fresh lime juice

1 tablespoon soy sauce

½ cup coarsely chopped cilantro

1 tablespoon sesame oil

½ cup olive oil

Salt and freshly ground black pepper

In a blender, combine the ginger, shallot, vinegar, lime juice, soy sauce, cilantro, and sesame oil. With the blender running, slowly drizzle in the olive oil to emulsify. Season with salt and pepper to taste. Store the vinaigrette in an airtight container in the refrigerator until ready to use. The vinaigrette will last up to 2 days before discoloring.

Denali Summit Soy Salmon
with Cilantro Coconut Chutney

Makes 4 servings

You won't actually find salmon at the summit of Denali, but I can't help thinking that this would make for a great celebration meal of such an accomplishment! Of course, this is an excellent meal for any occasion—feel free to make up your own celebration to go along with it.

> ¾ cup dark beer
>
> ½ cup soy sauce (I use the low-sodium version)
>
> 1 tablespoon canola oil
>
> 1 tablespoon fresh lemon juice
>
> 1 clove garlic, minced
>
> Dash sea salt
>
> Dash freshly ground black pepper
>
> 4 salmon fillets (about 6 ounces each), skinned and boned
>
> Cilantro Coconut Chutney (recipe follows)

Combine the beer, soy sauce, canola oil, lemon juice, garlic, salt, and pepper in a medium-size mixing bowl. Put the mixture in a shallow baking dish, and place the salmon in it. Marinate in the refrigerator for 30 minutes to 1 hour.

Lightly coat a gas or charcoal grill with cooking spray and heat the grill to medium-high. Discard the marinade and place the salmon on the grill. Cook for about 3 minutes on each side, or until the fish begins to flake.

Remove to a warm platter. Top with the chutney and serve with a nice brown rice or rice pilaf.

Cilantro Coconut Chutney

1 cup fresh cilantro leaves, tightly packed

⅓ cup shredded sweetened coconut

3 tablespoons water

Juice of 1 lime (about 2 tablespoons)

1 tablespoon minced seeded jalapeño

1 teaspoon minced peeled ginger

2 teaspoons curry powder

1 clove garlic, minced

Dash sea salt

In a food processor, combine the cilantro, coconut, water, lime juice, jalapeño, ginger, curry powder, garlic, and salt. Blend until fairly smooth (the mixture should still have a bit of coarseness). Store for up to 2 days in an airtight container in the refrigerator until ready to use.

Kenai Special Salmon with Prosciutto
and Saffron Tomato Salsa

Makes 4 servings

Saffron is an exotic spice as well as an expensive one. Difficult to obtain, saffron comes from the crocus flower, and it can take up to 4,000 flowers to make just 1 ounce. Expensive as it might be, the beautiful color and flavor it adds is well worth any cost. Serve this dish with basmati rice for a Mediterranean style.

> **4 salmon fillets (about 7 ounces each)**
>
> **Freshly ground black pepper**
>
> **4 thin slices prosciutto**
>
> **2 tablespoons olive oil**
>
> **2 cups cooked basmati rice, warm and ready to serve**
>
> **Saffron Tomato Salsa (recipe follows)**

Preheat the oven to 400°F.

Season the salmon to taste with black pepper. Wrap each salmon fillet in a slice of prosciutto, making sure that the seam is on the skin side of the salmon.

Heat the olive oil in a large oven-safe skillet until slightly smoking. Sear the salmon on the presentation side (the meat side), until a crust begins to form. Turn over to the skin side and place the skillet in the oven, cooking for 10 to 12 minutes (be careful not to overcook!).

Place the salmon fillets on a plate over basmati rice. Spoon the salsa over the top and serve immediately.

Saffron Tomato Salsa

2 tablespoons water

½ teaspoon saffron threads

½ cup diced white onion

2 cups diced tomatoes

Juice of 2 limes (about ¼ cup)

¼ cup diced red onion

1 to 2 jalapeños, seeded and minced

¼ cup chopped fresh cilantro

Salt and freshly ground black pepper

In a small saucepan, cook the water and saffron over low heat until the saffron color and flavor is evident. Add the white onion and remove from heat. Stir the onion until it has taken on the yellow color of the saffron. Transfer to a bowl and mix in the tomatoes, lime juice, red onion, jalapeños, and cilantro. Season to taste with salt and pepper.

Store the salsa in an airtight container in the refrigerator until ready to serve.

Prosciutto Apple Salmon
with Honey Mustard Vinaigrette

Makes 4 servings

I started out wrapping this salmon in prosciutto. It needed something for texture, so I came up with using apples. Make sure you use apples that are firm. Granny Smiths add a wonderful flavor to this exquisite fall dish.

4 slices prosciutto

1 apple, cored, peeled, and cut into ¼-inch-thick slices (see recipe note below)

4 fresh sage leaves

4 salmon fillets (about 7 ounces each)

Kosher salt and freshly ground black pepper

1 tablespoon olive oil

Honey Mustard Vinaigrette (recipe follows)

Fresh watercress

Coat the apple slices with lemon juice to prevent discoloration.

Preheat the oven to 350°F.

Lay the prosciutto out on plastic wrap or wax paper. In the center of each slice, place equal amounts of the apple. Top with the sage.

Lightly season the salmon fillets with salt and pepper to taste and place on top of the sage, flesh side down. Wrap the ends of the prosciutto around the salmon, pressing onto the skin side to seal.

Heat the olive oil in a nonstick, oven-safe sauté pan over medium-high heat. Sear the fish, skin side up, until a crust forms. Turn the fish over and put the pan in the oven for 8 to 10 minutes.

Arrange the watercress on 4 plates and place the salmon in the center. Drizzle with vinaigrette. Serve immediately.

Honey Mustard Vinaigrette

1 tablespoon minced peeled ginger

2 tablespoons chopped shallot

2 tablespoons rice vinegar

1 tablespoon stone-ground mustard

2 tablespoons honey

½ cup olive oil

Salt and freshly ground black pepper

Combine the ginger, shallot, vinegar, mustard, and honey in a blender. With the blender running, slowly drizzle in the oil to emulsify. Season with salt and pepper to taste.

Wildfire Smoked Salmon Hash

Makes 4 servings

The smoky flavor of this salmon hash evokes images of the haze we see every summer as Alaska deals with the wildfires our dry heat brings. This is such an easy and delicious recipe, good for a lunch or light dinner. Top with poached eggs, Chive Hollandaise Sauce (see page 148), and some green onion for a breakfast treat!

2 tablespoons olive oil

2 medium russet potatoes, peeled, diced, and blanched

½ cup diced red, yellow, and green bell peppers

½ cup diced onion

1 cup flaked smoked salmon (make sure all bones are removed)

2 teaspoons chopped fresh dill

Salt and freshly ground black pepper

Heat the olive oil in large nonstick skillet over medium-high heat. Add the potatoes and cook until they are heated through and beginning to crisp, about 5 minutes. Stir in the peppers and onion and continue cooking until just tender. Mix in the salmon and dill, cooking until heated through. Season with salt and pepper to taste.

Garnish as desired and serve immediately.

Pan-Seared Salmon with Horseradish Parmesan Crust

Makes 4 servings

Horseradish lovers, you are in for a real treat with this recipe. Even if you aren't a big horseradish fan, the addition of the Parmesan takes away some of the bite and mellows the flavor nicely. Serve with a rice pilaf or potatoes. For extra flavor, try serving this with my Chive Hollandaise Sauce (see page 148).

½ cup freshly grated peeled horseradish root

½ cup grated Parmesan cheese (4 ounces)

4 salmon fillets (about 7 ounces each)

Salt and freshly ground black pepper

2 tablespoons olive oil

In a small bowl, combine the horseradish and Parmesan. Season the salmon fillets with salt and pepper to taste, then press the horseradish-Parmesan mixture onto each side.

Heat the olive oil in a large skillet over medium heat until lightly smoking. Sear the salmon until a crust forms, about 4 minutes per side. Serve immediately.

Pistachio-Roasted Resurrection Bay Halibut

with Sweet and Sour Swiss Chard

Makes 4 servings

The great thing about halibut is that it is a mild enough fish that nearly anything complements it. The nutty pistachios coupled with the tang of the chard are an amazing combination for this halibut dish. You can easily substitute salmon or another white fish with this as well.

> **4 halibut fillets (about 7 ounces each)**
>
> **Salt and freshly ground black pepper**
>
> **2 tablespoons cornstarch**
>
> **2 eggs, whipped and diluted with 2 tablespoons water**
>
> **½ cup ground pistachios**
>
> **2 tablespoons olive oil**
>
> **Sweet and Sour Swiss Chard (recipe follows)**

Preheat the oven to 375°F.

Season the halibut fillets to taste with salt and pepper. Dust them lightly with the cornstarch, then dredge in the egg and lightly toss the fillets in the ground pistachios.

Heat the olive oil in a nonstick skillet over medium heat until a light haze forms. Put the fish in the skillet and sear, skin side up, until a crust begins to form. Turn and cook the other side, then remove the fillets from the skillet and place on a baking sheet.

Put the baking sheet in the oven and cook the fillets for 8 to 10 minutes, or until they reach the desired level of doneness. Remove to a serving plate and top with the chard. Serve immediately.

Sweet and Sour Swiss Chard

8 ounces bacon, cut into ¼-inch strips

1 cup julienne yellow onion

¼ cup apple cider vinegar

¼ cup firmly packed brown sugar

2 heads Swiss chard, tough stalk removed, rinsed, patted dry, and torn into 4-inch strips

Salt and freshly ground black pepper

In a medium-size skillet, cook the bacon until crisp and drain the excess fat. Add the onion, cooking and stirring until translucent, about 2 minutes. Stir in the vinegar and the brown sugar, cooking until the sugar is dissolved. Mix in the chard and heat through until it is just wilted (do not overcook or your chard will lose all its color and flavor).

Season with salt and pepper to taste and serve immediately.

Seward's Bounty Halibut Piccata

Makes 4 servings

Just a few hours outside of Anchorage is the coastal town of Seward, Alaska. This is a beautiful little fishing town, sitting right on Resurrection Bay. Halibut charters abound here, with some of the biggest fish on record caught by both tourists and locals. This dish gives a nod to the bounty of the bay. Serve with my Traditional Caesar Salad (see page 48) and perhaps some steamed rice. Top with lemon slices and chopped fresh parsley.

> **2 pounds halibut fillets, cut into 1-inch-thick pieces**
>
> **1 cup all-purpose flour, seasoned with salt and pepper**
>
> **4 to 6 tablespoons olive oil**
>
> **2 tablespoons capers**
>
> **1 tablespoon finely chopped garlic**
>
> **¼ cup white wine**
>
> **2 tablespoons fresh lemon juice**
>
> **¼ cup heavy cream**
>
> **¼ cup (½ stick) chilled unsalted butter, cut into small pieces**
>
> **Salt and freshly ground black pepper**

Preheat the oven to 200°F.

Dust the halibut with some of the seasoned flour and set aside.

Heat the olive oil in a large skillet over medium heat. Sear the halibut until it is lightly browned, about 4 minutes per side. Remove from the skillet and place in a baking dish, putting it in the preheated oven to keep warm.

Add the capers and garlic to the skillet. Pour in the wine and lemon juice, and cook for about 2 minutes, until the mixture is reduced by half. Stir in the cream and bring it to a boil, again cooking until the mixture reduces by half. Carefully swirl in the butter, moving the pan back and forth a bit to incorporate.

Remove the halibut from the oven, and drizzle the mixture over the fillets. Garnish with lemon slices and parsley and serve immediately.

Smoked Alaskan Salmon Bruschetta, *page 16*

Kincaid Grill's Seafood Fusion, *page 42*

Alaskan King Salmon with Arugula Pesto, *page 74*

Pistachio-Roasted Resurrection Bay Halibut with
Sweet and Sour Swiss Chard, *page 86*

Kodiak Roast Rack of Venison with Green Peppercorn Polenta, *page 112*

Coastal Hunter's Curry Lemongrass Duck, *page 130*

Roast Pork Tenderloin with Harvest Pumpkin Seed Pesto, *page 134*

City Diner Pineapple Upside-Down Cake, *page 174*

Peppered Halibut
with Ginger Butter

Makes 4 servings

The ginger butter added to the halibut gives it a nice kick, yet it is not overpowering. You can also easily prepare these fillets on a gas or charcoal grill. Serve over rice or a bed of mixed greens.

4 halibut fillets (about 5 ounces each)

1 tablespoon freshly ground black pepper

Kosher salt

2 tablespoons olive oil

Ginger Butter (recipe follows)

Season each halibut fillet with pepper, pressing it firmly into the flesh. Season with salt to taste. Prepare the ginger butter and set aside.

In a medium-size sauté pan, heat the olive oil over medium-high heat. Sear the halibut until a golden crust forms. Turn and cook the other side, until the fish is firm to the touch (about 3 to 4 minutes per side).

Remove the fillets and place on a warmed serving platter. Top with a scoop of the ginger butter right before serving.

Ginger Butter

½ cup (1 stick) unsalted butter, softened

2 teaspoons minced peeled ginger

1 teaspoon freshly ground black pepper

1 teaspoon minced garlic

Kosher salt

In a small bowl, mix together the butter, ginger, pepper, and garlic by hand until the mixture is smooth. Season with salt to taste. Store in an airtight container in the refrigerator for up to 1 week, or until ready to use.

Locals-Only Halibut Olympia

Makes 4 to 6 servings

This recipe is as old as Olympia itself. The first recipe I ever did with halibut was this one, way back when I first moved to Alaska in 1984. It has proven to be a timeless classic, as we Alaskans love our halibut, stashing fillets in our freezers to bring back a taste of summer during those long winters.

1 tablespoon olive oil

1 cup julienne yellow onion

1 cup mayonnaise

2 tablespoons fresh lemon juice

1 tablespoon Worcestershire sauce

¼ cup shredded Parmesan cheese (2 ounces)

Tabasco sauce

Salt and freshly ground black pepper

2 pounds halibut, cut into 4-ounce pieces

Topping

1 cup panko-style bread crumbs

½ cup (1 stick) unsalted butter, melted

1 tablespoon chopped fresh parsley

Preheat the oven to 375°F.

In a sauté pan, heat the olive oil over medium heat. Add the onion, cooking for about 3 to 5 minutes, or until it is just transparent. Set aside to cool completely.

In a small bowl, combine the mayonnaise, lemon juice, Worcestershire sauce, Parmesan, and a few drops of Tabasco. Mix by hand until smooth. Season with salt and pepper to taste.

Butter the bottom of a casserole and spread the onion evenly in the dish, seasoning with salt and pepper. Place the halibut fillets on top of the onion, and spoon the mayonnaise mixture evenly over the fillets.

In a another bowl, mix together the bread crumbs, butter, and parsley. Sprinkle it on top of the mayonnaise mixture. Put the casserole in the oven and bake for about 20 minutes, or until the topping is golden and slightly bubbly. Serve immediately.

Hawaiian Halibut, Alaskan Style

Makes 4 servings

I first created this dish with renowned Hawaiian chef Sam Choy as a guest on his show, Sam Choy's Kitchen. *Hawaii is perhaps the number-one vacation destination for Alaskans, so it is not surprising that we love any food that has island style! This recipe infuses Hawaiian regional cuisine with fresh Alaskan Halibut. For a beautiful presentation, serve over mixed greens and garnish with spicy, edible nasturtium flowers.*

2 tablespoons clarified unsalted butter (see recipe note on page 34)

4 halibut fillets (about 8 ounces each)

½ cup (1 stick) unsalted butter

4 ounces toasted macadamia nuts, crushed

½ cup citrus juice (any kind)

2 oranges, cut into 16 segments

1 lemon, cut into 16 segments

1 grapefruit, cut into 8 segments

Salt and freshly ground black pepper

Heat the clarified butter in a large skillet over medium-high heat. Sear the halibut on both sides until firm, about 4 minutes per side. Remove the fillets from the skillet and place on a warm platter.

In the same skillet, add the unsalted butter and cook until browned, stirring constantly and scraping up any bits from the bottom of the pan. Stir in the nuts and citrus juice. Remove from the heat and add the orange, lemon, and grapefruit segments, tossing lightly to coat. *Note:* Be careful not to add the fruit too soon, as the segments will break apart.

Divide the halibut among 4 plates and top with the citrus mixture. Season to taste with salt and pepper.

Halibut Amandine

Makes 6 servings

Local lakes in Anchorage are stocked seasonally with rainbow trout, the fish traditionally used in Amandine dishes. But being the catch-and-release sportsman that I am, I prefer to use halibut for this recipe. If you desire, you can use the traditional trout, but I've found halibut to be even more delicate and flavorful. This recipe brings out the distinct flavor of the fish, the nutty seasoning creating a wonderful accompaniment to your catch of the day.

6 halibut fillets (7 ounces each), or 6 whole trout, dressed with heads on

1 cup all-purpose flour, seasoned with salt and pepper

1 tablespoon vegetable oil

½ cup slivered almonds

Juice of 1 lemon (about 3 tablespoons)

½ cup (1 stick) unsalted butter, clarified (see recipe note on page 34)

2 tablespoons chopped fresh parsley

Salt and freshly ground black pepper

Dredge the halibut in the seasoned flour. Heat the vegetable oil in a large skillet over medium-high heat. Fry the halibut for about 4 minutes per side (5 minutes if you prefer your fish well-done), or until well browned. Remove the halibut to a warmed platter.

Add the almonds to the skillet, tossing lightly to toast. Stir in the lemon juice. Slowly mix in small amounts of the butter, until it takes on a nutty aroma. Add the parsley and season to taste with salt and pepper. Pour the sauce over the halibut and serve immediately.

Summer Sea Bass
with Saffron Tomato Sauce

Makes 4 servings

Sea bass is a long-living, slow-growing fish that is found in Arctic waters. It has a mild, buttery flavor that complements any recipe. This is a favorite of mine, very simple but elegant. Top it with a bit of chopped fresh parsley and serve with rice or pasta.

½ cup dry white wine

1 clove garlic, peeled and smashed

1 medium shallot, finely chopped

1 teaspoon finely grated lemon peel

½ teaspoon freshly ground pepper

Pinch fresh thyme

4 sea bass fillets (about 5 ounces each)

Saffron Tomato Sauce (recipe follows)

In a medium bowl, combine the wine, garlic, shallot, lemon peel, pepper, and thyme. Put in the fillets, turning to coat. Marinate the fillets in the refrigerator for 45 minutes or up to 2 hours.

Heat a gas or charcoal grill, or a broiler, to medium-high. Discard the marinade. Cook the fillets, turning once, for 3 to 4 minutes on each side, or until the fish is firm throughout.

Spoon the warm tomato sauce onto 4 serving plates and top with the fish fillets, garnishing with a bit of parsley.

Saffron Tomato Sauce

   1 tablespoon olive oil

   1 stalk celery, diced

   1 medium carrot, diced

   1 medium yellow onion, diced

   2 cloves garlic, peeled and smashed

   4 to 5 large ripe tomatoes, chopped and liquid reserved

   1¾ cups chicken stock (see Basic Stocks on page 25)

   Pinch saffron threads

   Dash pepper

   Fresh lemon juice

In a medium saucepan, heat the olive oil over medium-low heat. Cook the celery, carrot, onion, and garlic, covered but stirring occasionally, until the vegetables are tender, about 25 minutes.

Stir in the tomatoes, chicken stock, and saffron, and simmer uncovered until the mixture is reduced by half, about 30 minutes. Transfer to a food processor or blender and puree.

Season to taste with pepper and lemon juice. Serve immediately with the sea bass.

Specialty Meats and Grilling

Al's Grilled Leg of Lamb

City Diner Meatloaf

Winter Warmth Beef Stroganoff

Asian-Alaskan Fillet of Beef with Sesame and Spinach Watercress Stir-Fry

City Diner's Braised Beef Short Ribs with Wild Mushrooms
and Red Wine Gravy

Osso Buco

Endless Summer Grilled Bratwurst with Sauerkraut and Off-the-Grill Corn

Kodiak Roast Rack of Venison with Green Peppercorn Polenta

Marinated Grilled Buffalo Skewers with Shiitake Mushrooms

Wine is the intellectual part of a meal,
while meat is the material.

—ALEXANDRE DUMAS

WHILE WE ARE KNOWN FOR OUR SEAFOOD in Alaska, one should not forget about enjoying a good cut of meat. Up here, a subsistence lifestyle is still a reality for many people, and hunting season is an important time of year. A freezer full of moose meat, deer, or caribou means that a family has food all winter.

Of course, figuring out what to do with all that meat can be tough. There are only so many moose steaks one can fry up before it starts getting mundane. Having some versatility with cooking is vital when the choice for dinner is meat or more meat! Not to mention the fact that being able to create something new helps alleviate the potential boredom of those long winters.

We also love our barbecue grills, maybe because of those long winters. Summertime means being outside as much as possible, rain or shine. I've been known to stand in the rain on my back deck while cooking on the grill, simply because I know I don't have much time in the summer to enjoy it.

All of these recipes are versatile and can be used with any meat, so don't worry if it calls for deer and you want to use beef. Also, when cooking, remember that the firmer the meat is when you touch it, the more cooked it is. Don't let that nice cut of meat get overcooked!

Al's Grilled Leg of Lamb

Makes 4 to 6 servings (depending on the cut of meat)

Practice your butcher skills before attempting this one, or ask your butcher to break this down for you. You can also buy a boneless leg of lamb and it works just as well, while eliminating the need for excessive knife skills. Serve it with my Roasted Valley Vegetable Ratatouille (see page 154) and Poached Pear Salad with Fireweed Honey–Pepper Vinaigrette (see page 50).

½ cup chopped fresh rosemary

¼ cup chopped garlic

¼ cup soy sauce

2 tablespoons finely grated lemon peel

¼ cup olive oil

1 lamb leg, bone out and broken down

In a large bowl, combine the rosemary, garlic, soy sauce, lemon peel, and olive oil. Marinate the lamb in the mixture at room temperature for up to 2 hours.

Preheat a gas or charcoal grill on high. Discard the marinade and put the lamb on the grill, cooking 4 to 6 minutes per side, depending on the desired doneness. The key is to put the larger pieces on first and the smaller pieces on last, as not to over- or undercook the lamb.

City Diner Meatloaf

Makes 6 to 8 servings

This meatloaf recipe has become very popular at City Diner, the restaurant I co-own. I think it will become one of your family's favorites too. This recipe makes about two loaves, so feel free to cut it in half if you are serving fewer people.

2 tablespoons unsalted butter

2 cups finely diced yellow onion

1 tablespoon minced garlic

¼ cup finely diced celery

¼ cup finely diced carrot

½ cup chopped green onion (both white and green parts)

2 teaspoons salt

1½ teaspoons freshly ground black pepper

2 teaspoons Worcestershire sauce

1 cup ketchup

1½ pounds ground beef

¾ pound ground pork

1 cup bread crumbs

2 eggs, beaten

¼ cup chopped fresh parsley

1 tablespoon chopped fresh rosemary

Preheat the oven to 350°F.

In a large sauté pan, melt the butter over medium heat. Cook and stir the onion, garlic, celery, carrot, and green onion until crisp-tender, about 4 minutes. Stir in the salt, pepper, Worcestershire sauce, and half of the ketchup, cooking for about 1 minute more. Remove from the heat and cool to room temperature.

When the mixture has cooled, transfer it to a large mixing bowl. Using a wooden spoon, mix in the beef, pork, bread crumbs, eggs, parsley, and rosemary.

Using 2 loaf pans lightly coated with cooking spray, form the mixture into 2 loaf shapes and put in the pans. Top each loaf with the remaining ketchup. Place loaf pans in the center of the oven and cook for 40 to 60 minutes, or until the internal temperature of the meat reaches 155°F. Let rest for 15 minutes before serving.

Winter Warmth Beef Stroganoff

Makes 4 servings

As hearty as we Alaskans are, it seems as though we still spend a lot of time focusing on one thing during those long winters—keeping warm! This recipe will warm you through and through. It can also be prepared and placed in a slow cooker and kept on low until you are ready to serve. I've added caraway to this recipe (one of my favorite ingredients); the dill pickle adds a surprising wow factor.

1 pound beef tenderloin, well trimmed and cut into 2- by 1-inch strips

Salt and freshly ground black pepper

2 tablespoons vegetable oil

¼ cup finely chopped shallot

1 pound fresh button mushrooms, finely chopped

2 tablespoons brandy or cognac

3 tablespoons unsalted butter

2 tablespoons all-purpose flour

1 cup beef stock (see Basic Stocks on page 25)

¾ cup sour cream

1 tablespoon Dijon mustard

1 tablespoon chopped dill pickle

1 teaspoon caraway seeds

One 12-ounce package wide egg noodles

Paprika

Pat the meat dry with paper towels and sprinkle all over with salt and pepper. In a large skillet, heat the oil over high heat until very hot. Place the meat in the skillet in a single layer and cook just until brown on the outside, about 1 minute per side. Stir in the shallot and the mushrooms, cooking with the meat until all is cooked through, about 10 minutes.

Deglaze the skillet with the brandy, scraping up any bits from the bottom. Cook until the alcohol burns off, about 2 minutes, then mix in 2 tablespoons of the butter. Sprinkle lightly with the flour and stir to incorporate. Pour in the beef stock and bring it to a boil. Cook the mixture over medium heat for about 30 minutes, or until the flour taste is gone.

After it has simmered, stir in the sour cream, mustard, pickle, and caraway seeds. Cover and heat the mixture just to boiling, stirring occasionally, then reduce the heat to low until ready to serve. Season with salt and pepper to taste.

Meanwhile, bring salted water to a boil in a large stockpot. Cook the egg noodles until tender, about 8 minutes. Drain and transfer to a bowl. Add the remaining butter, tossing to coat. Season the noodles with salt and pepper and divide them among 4 plates. Top with the beef and sauce. Sprinkle generously with paprika.

Asian-Alaskan Fillet of Beef with Sesame
and Spinach Watercress Stir-Fry

Makes 4 servings

In this Asian-influenced dish, the red chiles give a bit of a kick without overpowering it. I really like the combination of spinach and watercress too. It's not too heavy and it is a very healthy vegetable dish. Top with sesame seeds and minced green onions. Serve with fluffy white rice.

> 4 cloves garlic, minced
>
> 1½ tablespoons soy sauce
>
> 1 tablespoon fish sauce
>
> 1 teaspoon sesame oil
>
> 1 tablespoon light brown sugar
>
> 1 teaspoon freshly ground black pepper
>
> 3 small red chiles, seeded and chopped
>
> 1 pound beef fillet, cut into ½-inch-thick slices
>
> 1 tablespoon peanut oil

In a small bowl, combine the garlic, soy sauce, fish sauce, sesame oil, brown sugar, pepper, and chiles. Marinate the beef overnight in a covered glass dish in the refrigerator.

Heat the peanut oil in a wok or sauté pan over high heat. Discard the marinade and quickly sear the beef in a single layer, until well browned, about 4 minutes per side.

Remove the beef to a warmed serving platter, garnish with sesame seeds and green onions, and accompany with the stir-fry.

Spinach Watercress Stir-Fry

1 pound fresh spinach, rinsed, patted dry, and shredded

2 bunches watercress, torn into pieces

1 tablespoon peanut oil

1½ tablespoons minced garlic

2 tablespoons fish sauce

In a medium-sized stockpot, bring 4 cups of lightly salted water to a boil. Blanch the spinach and watercress for just under 1 minute, until wilted and vivid green. Run them under cold water, then squeeze out as much excess water as possible. Set aside.

Heat the peanut oil in a wok or sauté pan and stir-fry the garlic until light brown. Add the greens and cook until heated through, about 1 minute. Splash the mixture with the fish sauce and serve immediately.

City Diner's Braised Beef Short Ribs with Wild Mushrooms and Red Wine Gravy

Makes 6 servings

This slow-cooked one-pot meal is a great choice for those chilly winter days when you are in need of comfort food. I just love the braising method of cooking, and this recipe has become a favorite at City Diner. The addition of caraway seed gives it a subtle but distinct flavor. Maybe it's because this recipe is a throwback to my German heritage, but I can't get enough of this dish.

¼ cup all-purpose flour

1 teaspoon ground allspice

12 meaty short ribs (3 to 4 inches long each), top membrane trimmed

Salt and freshly ground black pepper

4 tablespoons vegetable oil

3 large yellow onions, chopped

8 ounces fresh mixed specialty mushrooms, chopped into large pieces

3 large carrots, chopped

3 stalks celery, chopped

4 cloves garlic, minced

1 tablespoon dried thyme

2 teaspoons caraway seeds

3 bay leaves

3 cups beef stock (see Basic Stocks on page 25)

2 cups dry red wine

Combine the flour and allspice in a medium-size bowl. Season the short ribs with salt and pepper. Add 6 ribs to the flour mixture, turning to coat.

In a large stockpot, heat 3 tablespoons of the vegetable oil over medium-high heat. Add the ribs and cook and stir until brown, about 6 minutes, turning occasionally.

Transfer the ribs to a large bowl. Repeat the flouring and browning process with the remaining 6 ribs, reserving any remaining flour mixture.

Add the remaining vegetable oil to the pot. Cook the onions, mushrooms, carrots, and celery for about 30 minutes, or until they begin to brown and are very tender. Scrape the bottom of pot often.

Mix in the garlic, thyme, and caraway seeds, stirring for 1 minute. Drop in the bay leaves. Return the ribs and accumulated juices to the stockpot, arranging the ribs in a single layer. Pour in the beef stock and wine, bringing to a boil. Reduce the heat to medium-low and cover. Simmer until the short ribs are almost tender, about 1 hour.

Uncover and continue simmering for another 30 minutes, occasionally spooning fat from the surface (reserve 2 tablespoons of the fat). Combine the reserved flour mixture and reserved fat in a small bowl until a smooth paste forms. Stir the paste into the sauce all around the ribs. Simmer until the meat is tender and the gravy thickens, about 45 minutes longer. Season with salt and pepper to taste.

Osso Buco

Makes 2 servings

One of my favorite braised meat dishes, this Italian dish remains traditional with the use of gremolata, a lemon zest mixture that adds an amazing flavor to the veal. Though often imitated with lamb shank, true osso buco is made with veal. Serve with polenta or my Truffle Potatoes (see page 156).

   2 tablespoons olive oil

   2 veal shanks (12 to 14 ounces each)

   Salt and freshly ground black pepper

   2 cloves garlic, peeled and minced

   1 small carrot, diced

   1 stalk celery, diced

   ½ small yellow onion, diced

   ½ cup peeled, seeded, and diced tomatoes

   1 cup chicken stock (see Basic Stocks on page 25)

   1 sprig fresh thyme

   1 sprig fresh rosemary

   1 tablespoon freshly grated orange peel

   Gremolata (recipe follows)

Preheat the oven to 350°F.

In a large skillet, heat the oil over medium-high heat until smoking slightly. Season the veal with salt and pepper. Sear in the skillet until well browned, about 6 minutes per side. Remove the veal to a casserole.

In the same skillet, cook the garlic, carrot, celery, onion, and tomatoes for about 5 minutes. Deglaze with the chicken stock, scraping up any browned bits from the bottom. Bring the mixture to a boil, then add the thyme, rosemary, and orange peel. Pour the mixture over the veal shanks. Cover with foil and roast in the oven until tender, 1½ to 2 hours. Remove from the oven and put the veal shanks on a warmed platter.

Skim off any remaining cooking liquid from the casserole and pour back into the skillet, cooking over medium-high heat until slightly reduced. Pour the liquid over the shanks. Sprinkle with gremolata and serve immediately.

Gremolata

2 tablespoons chopped parsley

1 teaspoon chopped garlic

1 teaspoon finely grated lemon peel

In a small bowl, mix together the parsley, garlic, and lemon peel. Hold at room temperature until ready to use.

Endless Summer Bratwurst
with Sauerkraut
and Off-the-Grill Corn

Makes 4 to 6 servings

My old friend Hans Kruger shared this sauerkraut recipe with its addition of applesauce. My German sensibilities were stunned! I quickly created my own version and it's one of the best barbecue meals you can make. Add the corn as a side and you'll have a new family favorite.

> **4 to 6 bratwursts**
>
> **¼ pound bacon, cut into ¼-inch pieces**
>
> **½ cup diced yellow onion**
>
> **2 cups store-bought sauerkraut, rinsed and drained**
>
> **1 cup store-bought applesauce**
>
> **½ tablespoon caraway seeds**
>
> **Salt and freshly ground black pepper**

Heat a gas or charcoal grill to medium-hot and cook the bratwursts until browned and plump, about 15 to 20 minutes. *Note:* You can also use bratwursts that are precooked and simply heat through. Remove the bratwurst from the grill and set aside, placing on a warmed platter.

In a large skillet, cook the bacon until crisp, about 10 minutes. Drain off the fat until about 2 tablespoons remain. Stir in the onions and cook until translucent, about 2 minutes. Spoon in the sauerkraut, applesauce, and caraway seeds. Season to taste with salt and pepper.

Serve the mixture over the brats and with grilled corn.

Off-the-Grill Corn

¼ cup (½ stick) unsalted butter

Salt and freshly ground black pepper

4 to 6 ears of corn, husked and cleaned

Heat a gas or charcoal grill to medium-high. Using 4 to 6 sheets of aluminum foil, spread the butter on the dull side of the foil. Season the butter with salt and pepper to taste, and place the corn on the butter, wrapping up the foil to form a package.

Put the packages on the hot grill and turn every 3 to 4 minutes, until cooked through (about 15 minutes total). Keep warm on the upper racks of the grill until ready to serve.

Kodiak Roast Rack of Venison
with Green Peppercorn Polenta

Makes 4 servings

In Alaska we serve a lot of game recipes in our restaurants. The first time I tried this recipe I used buffalo medallions, but I soon decided that the presentation of the venison rack really made it pop. If you have access to fresh berries, such as blueberries or blackberries, they make a very nice garnish and give it a rustic Alaskan feel.

> **2 sprigs fresh rosemary**
>
> **2 cloves garlic, peeled and chopped**
>
> **1 tablespoon soy sauce (I use low sodium in this recipe)**
>
> **1 tablespoon fresh lemon juice**
>
> **¼ cup olive oil**
>
> **Kosher salt and freshly ground black pepper**
>
> **4 venison racks (about 12 ounces each)**
>
> **Green Peppercorn Polenta (recipe follows)**
>
> **Raspberry Vinaigrette (recipe follows)**

Preheat the oven to 350°F.

In a large bowl, combine the rosemary, garlic, soy sauce, lemon juice, and olive oil. Season with salt and pepper to taste. Marinate the venison in this mixture in the refrigerator for 20 to 30 minutes.

Heat a large skillet over medium-high heat. Discard the marinade and sear the venison for about 6 minutes on all sides to seal in the juices.

Transfer the venison to a roasting pan and roast in the oven until the meat reaches the desired doneness, about 15 to 20 minutes. For the best flavor, venison should be served medium-rare. Assemble the venison and polenta on plates and drizzle with the vinaigrette.

Green Peppercorn Polenta

2 cups chicken or vegetable stock (see Basic Stocks on page 25)

½ cup uncooked polenta

1 to 2 tablespoons green peppercorns in brine, drained

Salt and freshly ground black pepper

Pat of butter (optional)

Dash of heavy cream (optional)

Pour the stock into a small saucepan and bring to a boil. Mix in the polenta, stirring vigorously. Continue stirring until the mixture is thickened. Add the peppercorns and season with salt and pepper to taste. Thin with additional stock if it sets up too much.

Keep warm until ready to use. For added flavor, add a pat of butter and dash of heavy cream.

Raspberry Vinaigrette

½ cup fresh or frozen raspberries

¼ cup rice wine or raspberry vinegar

2 tablespoons honey

1 tablespoon Dijon mustard

1 tablespoon chopped fresh herbs (equal parts thyme, oregano, and sage)

1 tablespoon chopped shallot

1 cup olive oil

In a blender, combine the raspberries, vinegar, honey, mustard, herbs, and shallot. With the blender running, slowly drizzle in the olive oil. Use immediately or store in an airtight container in the refrigerator.

Marinated Grilled Buffalo Skewers with Shiitake Mushrooms

Makes 4 to 6 servings

You can substitute beef or other game meats in this recipe, but buffalo is so tender and juicy, it is truly ideal for grilling. You can also use the rosemary sprig as a skewer, which is a really fun presentation and gives this dish a rustic feel.

Game Marinade (recipe follows)

1 to 2 pounds buffalo rib eye, cut into 1-inch cubes

4 ounces fresh shiitake mushrooms, cut into quarters

Salt and freshly ground black pepper

2 sprigs rosemary

Reduced Balsamic (see recipe note on page 56)

Prepare the game marinade and marinate the buffalo pieces in a covered dish in the refrigerator for 24 hours.

Discard the marinade. Put alternating pieces of buffalo meat and mushrooms on wooden or metal skewers. *Note:* Soak wooden skewers in water for 20 to 30 minutes prior to using to prevent scorching. Use 3 to 4 pieces of meat per skewer. Season with salt and pepper to taste.

Heat a gas or charcoal grill to medium-high heat (or heat a cast-iron skillet over medium-high heat). Grill the skewers for about 4 minutes per side, or until the meat reaches the desired doneness. Strip the rosemary sprigs and sprinkle the fresh leaves over the dish. Drizzle with reduced balsamic and serve immediately.

Game Marinade

½ cup honey

½ cup soy sauce

½ cup sherry

3 tablespoons sesame oil

3 cloves garlic, minced

1 tablespoon freshly grated ginger

1 teaspoon salt

1 teaspoon freshly ground black pepper

Whisk together the honey, soy sauce, sherry, sesame oil, garlic, ginger, salt, and pepper in a bowl. Store the marinade in an airtight container in the refrigerator until ready to use, up to 1 week.

Poultry and Pork

Roast Chicken with Spring Asparagus and Tahini

Lemon Tarragon Roast Chicken with Tomato Confit

Greek-Alaskan Grilled Chicken Gyro with Cucumber Dill Sauce

Cheechako Chicken Roulade with Tomato Basil Supreme Sauce

Pancetta-Wrapped Chicken with Braised Lettuce Sauce

Paillard of Turkey Breast with Citrus, Field Greens,
and Toasted Walnut Vinaigrette

Coastal Hunter's Curry Lemongrass Duck

Lemon Herb Cornish Hen with Tabbouleh and Arugula Salad

Roast Pork Tenderloin with Harvest Pumpkin Seed Pesto

Marinated Grilled Pork Chops

Stuffed Pork Tenderloin

Pork Loin with Ancho-Anchorage Chipotle Rub and Apple Chutney

There is poetry in a pork chop to a hungry man.
—Philip Gibbs

PEOPLE TEND TO GET CARRIED AWAY when it comes to cooking poultry and pork. While the risks associated with eating these meats undercooked are very real, don't get so concerned that you end up with a dry, blackened chunk of pork that is inedible. The key is to cook the meat just until the juices run clear when pierced. The juice should not be pink, but it should still exist!

The great thing about a nice piece of chicken is that it tends to please even the pickiest eater. You can feel confident that your guests will be pleased with the taste of any of these recipes, and as always, none of them are overly difficult to prepare.

Most of these dishes can be substituted with fish as well, making for something unique. As I always say, don't be afraid to experiment. Make a recipe your own by tweaking it a bit and using different ingredients.

Roast Chicken with Spring Asparagus and Tahini

Makes 4 servings

Fresh spring asparagus combined with the mildly nutty taste of tahini is a perfect complement to classic roast chicken. Of course, you can substitute other vegetables if asparagus isn't available—fresh produce in Alaska is getting easier to find, but we can't always locate the items we want, so we learn to use whatever fresh veggies we can round up.

2 pounds fresh asparagus, trimmed and cut on a diagonal into 2-inch pieces

3 tablespoons olive oil

Salt and freshly ground black pepper

4 chicken breast halves, skinned, boned, rinsed, and patted dry

⅓ cup tahini

⅓ cup water

2 tablespoons fresh lemon juice

1 teaspoon granulated sugar

1 clove garlic, minced

Preheat the oven to 450°F.

In a medium bowl, toss the asparagus with 1 tablespoon of the olive oil and season to taste with salt and pepper. Set aside.

Season the chicken with salt and pepper. Heat the remaining olive oil in a non-stick skillet over medium-high heat. Cook the chicken, turning once, until golden (about 6 minutes total). Transfer the chicken to a large baking dish and top with the asparagus. Place the dish in the center of the oven and roast until just cooked through, about 8 minutes.

While the chicken is cooking, mix the tahini, water, lemon juice, sugar, and garlic in a blender until smooth. Add more water if the dressing is too thick. Place the chicken and asparagus on 4 plates, drizzling with the tahini dressing.

Lemon Tarragon Roast Chicken
with Tomato Confit

Makes 4 servings

This is another simple meal that has a flashy presentation. The lemon-tarragon combination is very flavorful, but it is not too intense or overpowering to the rest of the ingredients. The tomato confit really rounds out the flavor. Serve with my Truffle Potatoes (see page 156).

> 2 tablespoons chopped fresh tarragon
>
> 1 teaspoon minced garlic
>
> 2 tablespoons finely grated lemon peel (reserve the lemon)
>
> 4 chicken breast halves (about 6 ounces each), skin on, rinsed, and patted dry
>
> Kosher salt and freshly ground black pepper
>
> 2 tablespoons olive oil
>
> ½ cup white wine
>
> Tomato Confit (recipe follows)

Preheat the oven to 350°F.

In a small bowl, combine the tarragon, garlic, and lemon peel. Set aside. Lightly loosen the skin of the chicken by running your finger between the skin and the meat, forming a pocket. Divide the tarragon mixture and spread equal amounts under the skin of each chicken breast. Cut the reserved lemon and rub over the chicken; season with salt and pepper to taste.

Heat the olive oil in a large oven-safe skillet over medium-high heat. Carefully place the chicken, skin side down, in the pan and cook for about 3 minutes, or until well browned. Turn the chicken over and put the skillet in the oven, roasting until the juices run clear, about 15 to 20 minutes.

Remove the chicken and put the skillet back on the stovetop. Deglaze with the wine and tomato confit, scraping up any bits from the bottom of the pan. Heat through.

Slice the chicken and place on a serving platter, spooning the confit mixture around the chicken. Garnish as desired and serve immediately.

Tomato Confit

¼ cup olive oil

1 leek, rinsed, patted dry, and julienned

½ shallot, finely chopped

1 tablespoon minced garlic

4 roma tomatoes, cut into ½-inch-thick slices

½ cup julienne sun-dried tomatoes

¼ cup white wine

Kosher salt and freshly ground black pepper

Heat the olive oil in a sauté pan over medium heat. Stir in the leek, shallot, and garlic, cooking until tender, about 5 minutes. Add the roma tomatoes and sun-dried tomatoes, heating through. Pour in the wine and season with salt and pepper to taste.

Lower the heat and cook until the mixture is almost dry, about 5 minutes. Remove from the heat. This can be made up to 1 day in advance and stored in an airtight container in the refrigerator.

Greek-Alaskan Grilled Chicken Gyro
with Cucumber Dill Sauce

Makes 4 to 6 servings

The melting pot that is Alaska includes an influence of Greek culture. We have many restaurant owners who hail from Greece, and this dish gives a nod to their cuisine. I love the zesty flavor of the dill sauce, or tzatziki as it is properly called. This sauce is great on everything from meats to salads, so don't hesitate to use it with other dishes.

4 chicken breast halves (about 6 ounces each), skinned, boned, rinsed, and patted dry

2 tablespoons chopped fresh oregano

2 tablespoons chopped garlic

1 tablespoon finely grated lemon peel

4 tablespoons olive oil

1 medium tomato, cut into ¼-inch-thick rounds

1 medium red onion, cut into ¼-inch-thick slices

Chopped fresh herbs, such as thyme, oregano, parsley, and rosemary

Juice of 1 lemon (about 3 tablespoons)

Salt and freshly ground black pepper

1 package pita bread, warmed

Cucumber Dill Sauce (recipe follows)

In a large resealable plastic bag, combine the chicken, oregano, garlic, lemon peel, and 2 tablespoons of the olive oil. Seal the bag and pound the chicken using a mallet until it is fairly uniform in thickness. Marinate in the sealed bag in the refrigerator for 30 minutes (or overnight if desired).

In a small bowl, toss the tomato, onion, herbs, and lemon juice with 1 tablespoon of the olive oil. Season with salt and pepper to taste.

Heat a gas or charcoal grill to medium-high heat. Coat the grill with the remaining olive oil. Discard the marinade and grill the chicken until cooked through, about 7 minutes per side.

When the chicken is done, slice thinly and place on warm pita bread. Top with the tomato and red onion mixture. Spoon the dill sauce over all. Serve immediately.

Cucumber Dill Sauce

1 cup plain nonfat yogurt

½ cup peeled, seeded, and diced cucumber

1 tablespoon chopped fresh dill

1 clove garlic, minced

1 tablespoon fresh lemon juice

In a small bowl, combine the yogurt, cucumber, dill, garlic, and lemon juice. Store the sauce in an airtight container in the refrigerator for at least 8 to 12 hours to allow the flavors to blend.

Cheechako Chicken Roulade
with Tomato Basil Supreme Sauce

Makes 4 servings

In Alaska we call anyone who hasn't lived here through at least a few winters a "cheechako." This was originally a Canadian term coined by prospectors who came to Alaska during the Gold Rush. This chicken recipe is a great meal to help get one through those long winters—especially those first ones!

4 chicken breast halves (about 6 ounces each), skin on, boned, rinsed, and patted dry

4 slices Swiss cheese (about 6 ounces total)

4 slices ham (about 2 ounces each)

Tomato Basil Supreme Sauce (recipe follows)

Salt and freshly ground black pepper

Preheat the oven to 375°F.

Place each chicken breast in plastic wrap and pound lightly with a mallet until it is uniform in thickness and flattened to about 5 inches in diameter. Roll up the cheese and ham together and place on the chicken breasts. Roll the chicken up until it forms a pouch.

Take 4 sheets of aluminum foil and butter them lightly. Place the chicken on the foil, seam side down. Wrap each chicken breast tightly in foil. Place the foil packets in a large baking dish and roast in the oven for 25 to 30 minutes.

Remove the chicken from the foil, slice, and serve with the tomato basil sauce. Season with salt and pepper to taste.

Tomato Basil Supreme Sauce

1 tablespoon olive oil

1 roma tomato, diced

1 teaspoon chopped garlic

1 tablespoon chopped shallot

¼ cup white wine

¼ cup chicken stock (see Basic Stocks on page 25)

½ cup heavy cream

Salt and freshly ground black pepper

1 tablespoon chopped fresh basil

Heat the olive oil in a large skillet over medium-high heat. Stir in the tomato, garlic, and shallot, cooking for about 4 minutes or until translucent. Pour in the wine and cook until reduced by half. Pour in the chicken stock and continue reducing until the mixture is slightly thickened. Mix in the cream and cook until the sauce reaches desired consistency.

Season with salt and pepper to taste and add the basil. Drizzle over the chicken and serve.

Pancetta-Wrapped Chicken
with Braised Lettuce Sauce

Makes 4 servings

Versatile and easy, cooking with chicken is a snap because anything you pair it with is likely to taste great. This dish combines the smoky taste of pancetta with a very interesting lettuce sauce.

> **4 chicken breast halves (about 6 ounces each), skin on, rinsed, and patted dry**
>
> **4 large fresh basil leaves, with extra for garnish**
>
> **4 slices aged Gruyère cheese (about 4 ounces)**
>
> **4 strips pancetta**
>
> **Salt and freshly ground black pepper**
>
> **1 to 2 tablespoons olive oil**
>
> **Braised Lettuce Sauce (recipe follows)**

Preheat the oven to 350°F.

Lightly loosen the skin of the chicken breasts by running your finger between the skin and the meat, forming a pocket. Place the basil and Gruyère just under the skin. Wrap each chicken breast in pancetta and season with salt and pepper to taste.

Heat the olive oil in a large skillet over medium-high heat. Sear the chicken, skin side down, until well browned, about 5 minutes. Transfer the chicken, skin side up, to a large baking dish. Place in the oven and roast for 15 to 20 minutes, or until the juices run clear.

Prepare the braised lettuce sauce and spread over 4 plates. Top each with a chicken breast and basil for garnish. Serve with rice or a mixed green salad.

Braised Lettuce Sauce

¼ cup diced tomato

2 tablespoons chopped shallot

1 cup shredded iceberg lettuce

¼ cup dry white wine

1 cup heavy cream

Salt and freshly ground black pepper

In the same skillet the chicken was cooked in, cook the tomatoes, shallots, and lettuce over medium-high heat. Deglaze with the white wine, scraping up any bits from the bottom. Pour in the cream and allow the sauce to cook until just thick enough to coat a spoon. Season with salt and pepper to taste.

Paillard of Turkey Breast with Citrus, Field Greens,
and Toasted Walnut Vinaigrette

Makes 4 servings

"Paillard" is an old term used to describe cuts of meat that are thinly sliced or pounded into flattened pieces and cooked very quickly. You can purchase turkey cutlets that are already cut thin, or buy turkey breasts and pound them out yourself with a mallet.

Toasted Walnut Vinaigrette (recipe follows)

1 bunch field greens (such as arugula or watercress), rinsed and patted dry

1 grapefruit, peeled and cut into 6 segments

1 orange, peeled and cut into 6 segments

⅛ cup julienne red peppers

⅛ cup julienne yellow peppers

2 tablespoons chopped fresh herbs (equal parts thyme, sage, and basil)

2 tablespoons olive oil

4 turkey cutlets (about 5 ounces each)

Prepare the vinaigrette and toss in a large bowl with the field greens, grapefruit, orange, and red and yellow peppers.

In a small bowl, mix together the herbs with the olive oil. Heat the olive oil mixture in a skillet over medium-high heat. Quickly cook the turkey for about 2 minutes per side, or until just cooked through.

Arrange the field greens on a plate, top with the turkey, and drizzle with any remaining vinaigrette. Serve immediately.

Toasted Walnut Vinaigrette

½ cup walnuts

½ cup champagne vinegar

¼ cup honey

¼ cup sweet mustard

2 cups olive oil

Salt and freshly ground black pepper

Preheat the oven to 400°F.

Toast the walnuts by spreading them on a baking sheet and toasting in the oven for 4 to 6 minutes. In a blender, combine the walnuts, vinegar, honey, and mustard. With the blender running, slowly drizzle in the olive oil to emulsify. Season with salt and pepper to taste.

Coastal Hunter's Curry Lemongrass Duck

Makes 4 servings

An award winner at the University of Alaska's "One Pot" cooking competition, this dish is a showcase for the unique flavor of duck. One-pot cooking makes it an easy preparation. You will find most of the ingredients at any Asian market.

Duck Breast Marinade (recipe follows)

2 whole duck breasts, boneless with skin on

1 tablespoon vegetable oil

Salt and freshly ground black pepper

1 cup diced russet potato

6 lime leaves

1 to 2 tablespoons yellow curry paste

½ cup chicken stock (see Basic Stocks on page 25)

1½ cups coconut milk

1 pound raw jumbo shrimp (about 8), peeled and deveined

½ pound Alaskan sea scallops

½ cup julienne carrot

½ cup julienne red onion

½ cup finely chopped fresh Thai basil

½ cup coarsely chopped fresh cilantro

Dash granulated sugar

Dash fish sauce

2 tablespoons chili oil

2 tablespoons basil oil

Prepare the duck breast marinade. Marinate the duck in a covered dish in the refrigerator for about 1 hour.

Preheat the oven to 400°F.

In a 4-quart, cast-iron dutch oven, heat the vegetable oil over medium heat. Discard the marinade. Season the duck breasts with salt and pepper. Sear them quickly, about 6 minutes on the skin side and an additional 4 minutes on the other side, then stir in the potato, lime leaves, and curry paste, cooking in the fat rendered from the duck breasts. Pour in the chicken stock, deglazing the dutch oven by scraping up any browned bits from the bottom.

Pour in the coconut milk and bring the mixture to a simmer. Cook uncovered for about 10 minutes, or until the potato becomes tender. Stir in the shrimp, scallops, carrot, and onion, adding each at separate intervals so as not to overcook. Just before serving, stir in the basil and cilantro. Mix in the sugar and fish sauce to taste.

Place some shrimp and scallops on each plate and slice the duck breasts on the diagonal, fanning over the plate. Spoon the sauce and vegetables around the duck, and drizzle the chili oil and basil oil over the entire plate. Serve immediately.

Duck Breast Marinade

2 stalks lemongrass, pounded flat

2 julienne lime leaves

1 tablespoon fish sauce

1 tablespoon minced garlic

1 tablespoon fresh lime juice

1 tablespoon chopped fresh cilantro

In a small bowl, combine the lemongrass, lime leaves, fish sauce, garlic, lime juice, and cilantro. Store the marinade in an airtight container in the refrigerator until ready to use, up to 1 week.

Lemon Herb Cornish Hen
with Tabbouleh and Arugula Salad

Makes 4 servings

Tabbouleh is a Middle Eastern dish that is often served as an appetizer or salad. Thought to have originated in Lebanon, it is now enjoyed all over the world—even in Alaska! This savory salad is the perfect accompaniment to the tangy flavor of the Cornish hens.

4 whole Cornish game hens, rinsed and patted dry

2 tablespoons finely grated lemon peel

2 tablespoons chopped fresh herbs (equal parts oregano, thyme, and rosemary)

Olive oil

Juice of 1 lemon (about 2 tablespoons)

Salt and freshly ground black pepper

Preheat the oven to 375°F.

Lightly loosen the skin of the game hens by running your finger between the skin and the meat, forming a pocket. In a small bowl, mix together the lemon peel and the herbs. Divide the mixture evenly and place under the skin of each hen. Rub the hens with olive oil and squeeze the lemon juice over them. Season to taste with salt and pepper.

Place the hens in large roasting pan and roast for about 1 hour, or until the juices run clear. Allow the hens to rest for about 5 minutes, then split the hens and serve with the tabbouleh and arugula salad.

Tabbouleh and Arugula Salad

1 cup water

1 cup uncooked bulgur wheat

1 cup diced tomato

½ cup chopped arugula

½ cup diced red onion

¼ cup chopped fresh parsley

2 tablespoons chopped fresh mint

Juice of 1 lemon or lime (about 2 tablespoons)

2 tablespoons olive oil

Salt and freshly ground black pepper

Bring the water to a boil in a medium-size saucepan. In a large bowl, combine the bulgur wheat and the boiling water. Cover the bowl and allow the mixture to stand for 25 minutes.

Uncover and stir in the tomato, arugula, onion, parsley, mint, lemon juice, and olive oil. Season with salt and pepper to taste and toss well to combine. Mound the salad on a plate and serve at room temperature.

Roast Pork Tenderloin
with Harvest Pumpkin Seed Pesto

Makes 4 servings

This autumn dish is a fantastic alternative to the traditional turkey feast at Thanksgiving. Top with cilantro springs, pumpkin seeds, and olive oil. Serve with your favorite potato dish and a mixed green salad.

2 to 3 tablespoons Southwestern Pork Rub (recipe follows)

1 cup Harvest Pumpkin Seed Pesto (recipe follows)

½ cup Cranberry Vinaigrette (recipe follows)

2 pounds pork tenderloin, trimmed

2 tablespoons olive oil

1 bunch mixed field greens, rinsed and patted dry

1 apple (preferably a Macintosh), peeled, cored, and sliced

1 orange, peeled and cut into segments

1 fresh fig, cut into 4 wedges

¼ cup dried cranberries

Freshly ground black pepper

Prepare the pork rub, pumpkin seed pesto, and cranberry vinaigrette in advance and store in airtight containers in the refrigerator until needed. Remove the pesto from the refrigerator at least 30 minutes prior to use so that it can come to room temperature for best flavor.

Preheat the oven to 400°F.

Season the pork with the southwestern rub. In an oven-safe skillet, heat the olive oil over high heat. Sear the pork on all sides until nicely browned, about 5 minutes per side.

Put the pan in the oven and roast for about 20 minutes, or until the internal temperature reaches 150°F (for medium doneness). Remove from the oven and let it rest for 5 minutes.

Spoon the pesto onto a large serving platter or onto individual plates. Toss the mixed greens and the fruits with a small amount of olive oil and place on the platter. Slice the pork and arrange it adjacent to the greens. Drizzle the entire plate with the cranberry vinaigrette. Season with pepper to taste. Garnish as desired and serve.

Southwestern Pork Rub

1 tablespoon ground cumin

1 tablespoon ground chili powder

1 tablespoon garlic powder

1 tablespoon paprika

1 teaspoon ground cinnamon

1 tablespoon freshly ground black pepper

1 tablespoon kosher salt

In a small bowl, mix together the cumin, chili powder, garlic powder, paprika, cinnamon, pepper, and salt. This rub can be prepared several days in advance and is good for up to 1 month in an airtight container.

Harvest Pumpkin Seed Pesto

¾ cup green pumpkin seeds

¼ cup cold water

1 tablespoon chopped garlic

1 bunch cilantro, stemmed and coarsely chopped

2 green onions, minced (both white and green parts)

Juice of 1 lime (about 2 tablespoons)

Kosher salt and freshly ground black pepper

Toast the pumpkin seeds by placing them in a dry sauté pan and tossing lightly over medium-high heat until lightly brown. Remove the seeds immediately to a plate or paper towel and allow to cool.

(continued)

Combine the pumpkin seeds, water, garlic, cilantro, green onions, and lime juice in a food processor until a thick paste is formed. Do not overprocess—keep some texture. Transfer to a small glass bowl, and season with salt and pepper to taste. Cover the bowl with plastic wrap and store in the refrigerator. Bring to room temperature before serving. This pesto can be made up to 1 day in advance.

Cranberry Vinaigrette

½ cup whole-berry cranberry sauce

1 tablespoon minced peeled ginger

1 tablespoon minced shallot

¼ cup rice vinegar

Juice of 2 lemons (about ¼ cup)

½ teaspoon freshly ground pepper

1 cup vegetable oil (or any light oil)

Combine the cranberry sauce, ginger, shallot, vinegar, lemon juice, and pepper in a blender. With the blender running, slowly pour in the vegetable oil to emulsify. This can be prepared up to 1 day in advance. Store in an airtight container in the refrigerator.

Marinated Grilled Pork Chops

Makes 4 servings

Marinate these chops overnight for extra flavor. Easy to prepare on a gas or char-coal grill, these chops can also be cooked in a large sauté pan. I love them with a nice salad and a glass of white wine.

4 thick-cut pork chops (about 10 ounces each)

Salt and freshly ground black pepper

1 cup soy sauce

¼ cup firmly packed light brown sugar

2 tablespoons freshly ground black pepper

1 tablespoon chopped garlic

¼ cup diced fresh cilantro

½ cup olive oil

Pat the chops dry and season them lightly with salt and pepper to taste. In a medium bowl, whisk together the soy sauce, brown sugar, pepper, garlic, cilantro, and olive oil, until combined.

Pour the mixture into a large resealable plastic bag. Add the chops, seal the bag, and turn to coat with the mixture. Marinate the chops in the refrigerator for 30 minutes, or up to 24 hours.

Heat a gas or charcoal grill to medium-high. Discard the marinade and cook the chops until the juices run clear, about 4 minutes per side. Serve immediately.

Stuffed Pork Tenderloin

Makes 4 servings

Pork is a very versatile meat that has a mild flavor and complements almost any dish. This recipe makes for a hearty meal that isn't too detrimental to the waistline. I like to serve it with a fresh salad and a hearty side like potatoes.

1½ to 2 pounds pork tenderloin, silver skin removed

2 tablespoons olive oil

1 tablespoon chopped shallot

1 tablespoon chopped garlic

½ pound fresh mushrooms (any variety), chopped

1 cup cooked spinach (or thawed frozen chopped spinach, squeezed dry)

2 teaspoons chopped fresh thyme

1 teaspoon finely chopped fresh rosemary

1 tablespoon chopped fresh parsley

Salt and freshly ground black pepper

Fresh bread crumbs

How to select and prepare pork tenderloins: At your local butcher, try to find tenderloins that are large and fat rather than small and slender. This will make for ease in the stuffing process. Trim the tenderloin, removing the silver skin. Leave a bit of fat on the loin to keep it moist during roasting. Using a sharpening steel or boning knife, cut a hole through the center of the loin, trying not to split the sides in the process. Once a hole is through the middle, widen it out a bit by slitting the inside walls to allow for more stuffing. Set aside in the refrigerator until needed.

Preheat the oven to 350°F.

Prepare the pork tenderloin for stuffing as in the recipe note above.

In a large skillet, heat the olive oil over medium heat. Cook the shallot and garlic for about 2 minutes, stirring until translucent. Add the mushrooms, cooking until just tender, then gently stir in the spinach and heat through. Remove from the heat.

Season with the thyme, rosemary, parsley, salt, and pepper to taste. Put the mixture in a food processor and run until a smooth chopped consistency is achieved. Mix in the bread crumbs, just enough to absorb any excess liquid. Allow the mixture to cool in the refrigerator prior to stuffing.

Spoon the stuffing into a pastry bag fitted with a plain metal tip (a plastic bag with the corner cut off also works just fine). Retrieve the prepared pork loin from the refrigerator. Insert the tip of the pastry bag as far as possible into one end of the pork loin and carefully squeeze to push the stuffing into the center of the loin. Repeat this process on the opposite end until the loin is completely stuffed.

Season with salt and pepper, place in a large roasting pan, and roast in the oven for 25 to 35 minutes, or until the internal temperature reaches 160°F.

When the pork is finished cooking, allow to rest for 5 minutes before slicing. Cut the loin into medallions and serve on a warm platter with your favorite sauce or gravy.

Pork Loin with Ancho-Anchorage Chipotle Rub
and Apple Chutney

Makes 8 to 10 servings

While Alaska doesn't get the true autumn months that other states do, we enjoy clear, crisp days through the month of September and sometimes through October, at least until the snow flies. There is nothing quite like the combination of pork and apples to make one think of harvest time, even up here in the north where the fall season is short-lived.

> **2 pounds pork tenderloin, trimmed**
>
> **3 tablespoons olive oil**
>
> **¼ teaspoon salt**
>
> **1 teaspoon freshly ground black pepper**
>
> **6 cloves garlic**
>
> **2 tablespoons ancho-chipotle seasoning (available at most grocery stores)**
>
> **Apple Chutney (recipe follows)**

Preheat the oven to 500°F.

Heat a large nonstick skillet over medium heat. Rub the tenderloins with 1 teaspoon of the olive oil. Sprinkle the loins with the salt and pepper. Sear all sides in the hot skillet until browned, about 5 minutes on each side. Remove the pork from the skillet and put it in a roasting pan with a wire rack.

Using a mortar and pestle (or a food processor), grind the garlic and the ancho-chipotle seasoning. Slowly drizzle in the remaining olive oil to create a spreadable paste. Rub the paste all over the pork. Place the roasting pan in the center of the oven and roast until the internal temperature reaches 140°F.

Allow the cooked pork to rest for 10 minutes before carving. Carve the pork into 4-ounce portions (the size of your palm) and top each with ¼ cup of the apple chutney.

Apple Chutney

1½ pounds apples, peeled, cored, and coarsely chopped

1 tablespoon minced peeled ginger

¾ cup firmly packed light brown sugar

¼ cup white wine vinegar

½ teaspoon ground cinnamon

½ teaspoon mustard seeds

Pinch ground cloves

1 cup chopped yellow onion

⅓ cup currants or raisins

½ teaspoon salt

In a large saucepan, combine the apples, ginger, brown sugar, vinegar, cinnamon, mustard seeds, cloves, onion, currants, and salt. Heat the mixture over high heat until the sugar melts and begins to boil. Stir well, then reduce the heat to medium. Cook until the liquid has reduced to a thick syrup, with the apples very tender and the onion translucent, about 40 minutes.

Remove the chutney from the heat and allow it to cool to room temperature. This can be stored in the refrigerator, covered, for up to 1 month.

Sauces and Sides

Warm Tomatillo Vinaigrette

Red Wine Vinaigrette

Asian Inspiration Citrus Soy Sauce

Chive Hollandaise Sauce

Oils

Leek and Tarragon Stuffing

Roasted Valley Vegetable Ratatouille

Wild Mushroom Pasta

Truffle Potatoes

Red Chile Rice

Sleeping Lady Saffron Risotto

Woe to the cook whose sauce has no sting.
—Geoffrey Chaucer

IN FINE RESTAURANTS AROUND THE WORLD, the "saucier" or "sauce chef" is one of the most prestigious positions held in a kitchen. Responsible for creating the sauces and sautés, the saucier is usually subordinate only to the chef and sous-chef.

The high regard of the sauce chef gives a big indication of the importance of sauces in cooking. The right sauce can make or break your meal. The sauce recipes in this chapter are especially wonderful because they complement such a wide variety of dishes. Add in the array of easy side dishes I've provided and you can mix and match to your heart's content. These sides will even stand alone as entrées, although the addition of meat or seafood makes for a more complete dinner.

Remember to keep those ingredients fresh and to be open to experimentation. Many of the sauces can be made ahead; just make sure you store them as instructed.

Warm Tomatillo Vinaigrette

Makes 4 servings

This is another sauce that is wonderful over anything. Try it with roasted chicken or grilled fish. I've even been known to pour a bit over potatoes or rice—it's just that good.

½ cup olive oil

½ shallot, finely chopped (about 2 tablespoons)

4 fresh tomatillos, finely diced (husk and core removed)

2 cloves garlic, finely chopped

2 green chiles, roasted, peeled, seeded, and cut into ¼-inch strips

2 roma tomatoes, finely diced

Juice of 3 limes (about ¼ cup)

Minced fresh jalapeño

Chopped fresh cilantro

Kosher salt

In a large saucepan, heat the olive oil over medium-high heat. Stir in the shallot, tomatillos, and garlic, cooking until the garlic is lightly browned but not burned. Mix in the green chiles and tomatoes, cooking until heated through. Pour in the lime juice.

Season to taste with the jalapeño, cilantro, and salt. Set aside at room temperature until ready to use, then warm over medium heat right before serving.

Red Wine Vinaigrette

Makes 4 to 6 servings

Quick and easy, this vinaigrette goes with anything. Great on salads and amazing drizzled over steaks or seafood, it will replace your store-bought dressings. Why should you use something from a bottle when the homemade version is so simple and so much better?

1 tablespoon stone-ground mustard

½ shallot, finely chopped (about 2 tablespoons)

1 teaspoon minced garlic

½ cup red wine vinegar

1½ cups extra virgin olive oil

In a blender, combine the mustard, shallot, garlic, and vinegar. With the blender running, slowly pour in the olive oil to emulsify. Store the vinaigrette in an airtight container in the refrigerator until ready to use (it will last 1 week).

Asian Inspiration Citrus Soy Sauce

Makes 4 servings

This sauce is excellent with any fish or seafood. Serve warm, drizzling over the dish right before serving. I don't recommend making this one too far in advance, as the flavors will get too intense the longer it sits. Top with sesame seeds, fresh cilantro, orange segments, and red chiles.

2½ cups fresh orange juice

Juice of 1 lemon (about 3 tablespoons)

Juice of 1 lime (about 2 tablespoons)

¾ cup soy sauce

1 tablespoon rice vinegar

1 tablespoon sesame oil

1 tablespoon minced peeled ginger

Combine the orange juice, lemon juice, lime juice, soy sauce, vinegar, sesame oil, and ginger in a small saucepan. Stir and cook over medium heat for about 10 minutes. Pour the mixture through a strainer. Keep warm until ready to serve. Mix together the garnish ingredients and toss lightly, serving over the top of the sauce.

Chive Hollandaise Sauce

Makes 4 servings

This sauce does require a certain level of patience and finesse, but the end result is well worth it. A good hollandaise, smooth and redolent with butter, is a wonderful finish to a varitey of dishes. I've added a kick to the traditional recipe with chives and a dash of cayenne pepper.

4 egg yolks

1 teaspoon cold water

1 cup clarified unsalted butter (see recipe note on page 34)

2 tablespoons minced chives

2 tablespoons fresh lemon juice

Pinch cayenne pepper

Kosher salt

The secret to a perfect hollandaise sauce is taking your time. If you follow these directions exactly, your hollandaise should not curdle. But if it does, don't despair! Finish adding the butter as best you can, then remove the sauce to a small bowl, clean the pot, and start again with a fresh egg yolk. Begin the process again, using the curdled sauce as you would the butter.

Set a small, stainless-steel bowl in a heavy-bottomed pan, or use a heavy double boiler. Off the heat, put the egg yolks and cold water into the bowl (or in the top of the double boiler) and whisk until very well blended. Do not beat the mixture—stir evenly and continuously.

Place hot water in the pan (or bottom of the double boiler) and put the bowl or top of double boiler over it. If using a bowl, there should be about 1½ inches of water in the pan; with a double boiler the water should not touch the top section. Stir the eggs continuously, and slowly bring the water to a simmer. *Do not allow it to boil.* Continue stirring, ensuring there is no film at the bottom of the pan.

When the eggs have reached the consistency of heavy cream, slowly begin to add the butter with one hand while stirring vigorously with the other. Make sure each addition is fully added to the eggs before more is added. When all the butter has been added, stir in the chives. Then add the lemon juice a drop at a time, continuing to stir the mixture until it is completely blended. Add a pinch of cayenne pepper and season with salt to taste.

Oils

Making infused oils is quite easy and really can add to the looks and flavor of a dish. Drizzle over a fish dish just before serving, or place a few drops around the rim of a dinner or soup plate for a very nice appearance. The most important thing to remember is to stick to a neutral, mild oil that won't congeal in the refrigerator. Canola oil or a soybean salad oil work best.

Basil Oil

¾ cup fresh basil leaves

2 cups oil

Use cilantro leaves in place of basil leaves for cilantro oil.

Boil enough water to cover the leaves in a small saucepan. Place the basil in the pan, blanching for about 20 seconds. Remove the basil to a bowl of ice water to stop the cooking process. Squeeze out the excess water from the basil. Put the basil and oil in a blender and puree until smooth. Strain the mixture through a piece of cheesecloth (do not force the mixture through—set it aside and let it drain slowly) then store in refrigerator. Can be stored for up to 1 week.

Lemon Oil

5 lemons

1 cup vegetable oil

Warm the vegetable oil in a small pan or dish. Be sure not to overheat; you should be able to touch the oil without burning yourself. Zest the lemons and place the zest in the oil. Cover tightly with plastic wrap and let the mixture sit overnight—no need to refrigerate. Can be stored for up to 2 weeks.

Chili Oil

½ cup sambal oelek chili paste (available in most Asian markets)

2 cups oil

Puree the chili paste with the oil in a blender until well combined. Strain the mixture through a piece of cheesecloth (do not force the mixture—set aside and allow it to drain slowly). Store in the refrigerator until ready to use. Can be stored for up to 2 weeks.

Leek and Tarragon Stuffing

Makes 8 servings

Occasionally my wife, Raine, deigns to grace the kitchen with her presence. Although this recipe is of unknown origins, I consider it hers and it continues to be my favorite part of the traditional holiday meal. If you aren't into stuffing turkeys, you can also cook this one in a baking dish on its own, cooking at 350°F for about 40 minutes.

1 loaf buttermilk bread, crusts trimmed, and cut into ½-inch cubes (about 11 cups)

1 pound bacon, cut into 1-inch cubes

2 large leeks, rinsed, patted dry, and chopped (about 7 cups, white and pale green parts only)

1½ pounds fresh button mushrooms, coarsely chopped

¾ pound fresh shiitake mushrooms, stemmed and coarsely chopped

4 cups coarsely chopped celery

3 tablespoons chopped fresh tarragon (or 1½ tablespoons dried tarragon)

Salt and freshly ground black pepper

2 eggs, beaten

Chicken stock (see Basic Stocks on page 25)

Preheat the oven to 350°F.

Put the bread cubes on 2 large baking sheets and cook in the oven until dry, about 15 minutes. Remove and let cool, then transfer to a large bowl.

Cook the bacon in a large stockpot over medium-high heat until crisp. Remove the bacon and transfer it to paper towels to drain. Reserve 6 tablespoons of the bacon drippings in the stockpot and discard the remainder.

Stir in the leeks and button mushrooms, cooking until softened. Mix in the shiitake mushrooms and stir for another 3 to 4 minutes. Add the celery, continuing to cook until the mushrooms are tender but the celery is still slightly crisp, about 6 minutes. Add the tarragon and season generously with salt and pepper to taste.

Add the leek mixture to the bread crumbs. Fold in the eggs and mix well again. Allow to cool completely before stuffing the turkey.

Roasted Valley Vegetable Ratatouille

Makes 4 servings

This side works with almost any veggie combination and it is very easy to pre-pare. Fresh vegetables from the Mat-Su valley farms are always a great choice. When dicing, you will want to cut to about ½ inch.

½ cup diced eggplant

½ cup diced red, yellow, and green bell peppers

½ cup diced zucchini, unpeeled

½ cup diced red onion

½ cup diced yellow squash, unpeeled

2 large tomatoes, cut into 8 wedges

1 tablespoon olive oil

Salt and freshly ground black pepper

1 tablespoon chopped fresh herbs (equal parts basil, oregano, thyme, and parsley)

Balsamic vinegar, for drizzling

Preheat the oven to 450°F.

In a mixing bowl, coat the eggplant, bell peppers, zucchini, onion, yellow squash, and tomatoes with olive oil. Season to taste with salt and pepper.

Spread the mixture evenly on a baking sheet and roast in the oven until the edges brown, about 8 to 10 minutes. Stir in the herbs and drizzle with balsamic vinegar. Serve immediately.

Wild Mushroom Pasta

Makes 4 to 6 servings

This side is a great accompaniment for nearly any dish, from fish to meat. Use your favorite mushrooms—any variety works fine. Top with chopped fresh parsley. Don't go picking mushrooms out of your yard, though, unless you are very sure of what you are getting.

2 tablespoons olive oil

¼ pound fresh specialty mushrooms, chopped

2 tablespoons chopped garlic

¼ cup chicken stock (see Basic Stocks on page 25)

3 cups heavy cream

4 egg yolks

¾ cup grated Parmesan cheese (about 6 ounces)

Salt and freshly ground black pepper

1 pound fresh pasta (any shape), cooked

In a large skillet, heat the olive oil over medium heat until a light haze appears. Cook the mushrooms and garlic for about 5 minutes. Deglaze the skillet with the chicken stock, scraping up any browned bits from the bottom.

In a separate bowl, whisk together the heavy cream and egg yolks, mixing until smooth. Pour the mixture into the skillet and heat to just before the boiling point. Stir in the Parmesan and season with salt and pepper to taste.

Toss with the pasta, garnish as desired, and serve immediately.

Truffle Potatoes

Makes 4 servings

Truffle oil has a very rich flavor that adds immense depth to foods. It's an expensive oil, but a little goes a long way and it can be stored for a long time in your kitchen. This potato recipe complements any meat or poultry.

1 pound Yukon Gold potatoes, peeled and boiled (keep hot)

½ cup heavy cream

2 tablespoons unsalted butter

2 teaspoons truffle oil

Salt and freshly ground black pepper

Using an electric mixer, combine the potatoes, cream, butter, and truffle oil until smooth, about 4 minutes. Adjust the truffle oil to taste. Season with salt and pepper to taste. Serve immediately.

Red Chile Rice

Makes 4 servings

Touching on that Asian flair again, this side works well with chicken, fish, or pork. I really like it with seafood. Watch the spice on this one—those chiles will add heat quickly! I recommend you start slow and add more chiles to suit your personal taste.

1 tablespoon unsalted butter

1 tablespoon olive oil

¼ cup diced yellow onion

¼ cup diced red bell pepper

1 cup uncooked basmati rice

2 cups chicken stock (see Basic Stocks on page 25)

3 to 4 dried red chiles, seeded and crushed

Heat the butter and olive oil together in a large skillet over medium heat. When the butter has melted, stir in the onion and pepper, cooking until tender, about 3 minutes.

Mix in the rice, tossing slightly to coat with the butter-vegetable mixture. Continue cooking until the rice is lightly toasted, about 2 minutes. Pour in the chicken stock and drop in the chiles.

Bring to a boil, then cover and reduce the heat to low, cooking until the rice is tender and all the stock has been absorbed, about 20 minutes. Serve immediately.

Sleeping Lady Saffron Risotto

Makes 4 servings

Mount Susitna, or "Sleeping Lady" as she is locally known, overlooks Anchorage and is part of our folklore. According to the legend, a race of giants once lived in Alaska. Two young giants fell in love. One day there was word of an invading warrior group coming their way. The young man went with the other men of the village to meet the group and try to stop them. He told his love to wait for him by the water, known today as the Knik Arm, and he would come to her when he returned. For many days she waited faithfully. Eventually she fell asleep beside the water. News reached the village that the young man had been killed in a battle with the invading tribe. The women of the village could not bear to wake the young girl who slept so peacefully, waiting for her lover. So they left her there and she still slumbers today.

2 tablespoons olive oil

¼ cup diced yellow onion

1 cup uncooked arborio rice

2 to 2½ cups chicken stock (see Basic Stocks on page 25)

Pinch saffron threads

Heavy cream

Freshly grated Parmesan cheese

Salt and freshly ground black pepper

Heat 1 tablespoon of the olive oil in a large saucepan over medium heat. Stir in the onion, cooking until it is translucent, about 2 minutes. Mix in the rice and the remaining olive oil, stirring until heated through. Pour in enough chicken stock to cover the rice. Bring it to a slow boil and add the saffron.

Cook over medium heat until the stock absorbs. Pour in more stock, a little at a time, until the rice begins to look smooth and creamy and become tender. *Note:* The amount of stock will vary due to cooking temperature and brand of arborio. When the rice is just done, remove from the heat and spread it evenly on a baking sheet to slow the cooking process. Let it cool.

In a large sauté pan, heat a small amount of olive oil over medium heat; add the risotto, cream to cover the top of the risotto, and Parmesan to taste. Cook the mixture until the cheese and cream are well blended and the risotto takes on a nice creamy, thick consistency. Pour in more cream or chicken stock to achieve the desired consistency.

Season with salt and pepper to taste. Serve immediately.

Dessert Central

Ganache with Panache

Al's Butter Lace Cookies

Ginger Florentine Cookies

Arctic Valley Blueberry Bread Pudding

Cold Winter Night Flourless Chocolate Cake

Susitna Apple Rosemary Sorbet

Best of Anchorage Crème Brûlée

Harvest Pumpkin Crème Brûlée

Chocolate and Apricot Crepes

City Diner Pineapple Upside-Down Cake

Winter Wonderland White Chocolate Cheesecake

Wild Blueberry Rhubarb Tarts

Life is uncertain. Eat dessert first.
—Ernestine Ulmer

I'LL ADMIT IT: I'm not much of a dessert maker. The science of baking can be a challenge to even the most accomplished chef, and I am not too proud to say that it sometimes challenges me too! But that is really to your benefit, because these dessert recipes are straightforward and easy to create, with the finished products giving an elegant appearance that belies their simplicity.

These are some of my personal favorites, for while I might not be a dessert maker, I'm certainly a dessert eater. Some of these are variations on old family recipes that you might even remember your own mom or grandma making. Some of them have a modern, elegant style that guests will love.

No matter if you're making dessert for family or for a party, dinner just doesn't seem complete without something sweet as a finish. Served with espresso or tea, these recipes are the perfect way to close a meal.

Ganache with Panache

Makes 6 to 8 servings

Ganache is a relatively simple chocolate sauce that can be used over ice cream, cakes, or some beautiful fresh berries. It adds a nice touch to just about any dessert.

> **2 cups heavy cream**
>
> **¼ cup granulated sugar**
>
> **2½ cups bittersweet (not unsweetened) chocolate (about 20 ounces), chopped**

In a medium saucepan, combine the cream and sugar. Cook over medium heat until the sugar is completely dissolved, stirring constantly. Remove from the heat and add the chocolate, stirring vigorously until well combined.

This can be stored in an airtight container in the refrigerator and reheated for later use just before serving. It will keep for up to 2 weeks.

Al's Butter Lace Cookies

Makes 6 to 8 large cookies

These cookies are fun because you can shape them into a cone or bowl while they are warm. Fill with your favorite fruit or ice cream and drizzle with chocolate or raspberry sauce. Kids of all ages love them, and they make for a charming, edible conversation piece after dinner.

> 1 cup (2 sticks) unsalted butter, softened
>
> 1½ cups granulated sugar
>
> 1 tablespoon honey
>
> ½ tablespoon orange juice concentrate
>
> ⅔ cup all-purpose flour
>
> 1 teaspoon finely grated orange peel

Preheat the oven to 325°F.

Using an electric mixer, beat together the butter and sugar until well combined. Mix in the honey, orange juice concentrate, flour, and orange peel.

Form the dough into 1½-inch balls and put them on a nonstick baking sheet, pressing the dough with the back of a spatula to form large, flattened circles. Bake in the oven until slightly browned, about 8 to 10 minutes.

Ginger Florentine Cookies

Makes 2 dozen cookies

These are another variation of cookies you can shape into cones or bowls. I like this version because I really enjoy the addition of ginger—it adds a little kick to the overall flavor of the cookies. Add ice cream and drizzle with caramel and some shaved candied ginger for a lovely presentation.

> 3½ cups firmly packed brown sugar
>
> 1 cup (2 sticks) unsalted butter, melted
>
> 2 cups rolled oats
>
> 1½ cups all-purpose flour
>
> 1 tablespoon ground ginger
>
> 1 cup light corn syrup

Preheat the oven to 300°F.

Using an electric mixer, combine the brown sugar and butter in a large bowl. Mix in the oats, flour, and ginger. Pour in the corn syrup, mixing until fairly smooth.

Scoop out balls with a 1-ounce scoop (or use a spoon and shape into balls by hand). Put them on a nonstick baking sheet. With damp fingertips, press the balls out into flat circles, making them as thin as possible. Place the baking sheet in the center of the oven and cook for about 10 minutes.

Remove and let cool slightly, then drape each cookie over the end of a small cup or a bowl to make the ends curl up. Store the cookies in an airtight container until ready to use.

Arctic Valley Blueberry Bread Pudding

Makes 6 servings

Just outside of downtown Anchorage is the recreational area of Arctic Valley. A great place for skiing in the winter and golfing in the summer, the valley brings another enjoyable activity in the fall: picking the wild blueberries that blanket the surrounding hills and trails. A big scoop of ice cream or some freshly whipped cream rounds out the tang of the berries in this recipe.

8 cups heavy cream

1 vanilla bean, cut open and scraped

1¾ cups granulated sugar

8 egg yolks

1 loaf sourdough bread, torn into bite-size pieces

1 teaspoon ground cinnamon

½ teaspoon ground nutmeg

2 cups blueberries

2 tablespoons confectioners' sugar

½ cup (1 stick) unsalted butter, cut into pieces

Preheat the oven to 300°F.

In a large saucepan, heat the cream, vanilla bean, and granulated sugar over medium heat. Cook the mixture until the cream is just scalded, then remove from the heat. Allow the liquid to cool, then add the egg yolks. Pour the mixture through a strainer and set aside.

Put the sourdough pieces in a large mixing bowl. Pour the cooled batter into the bowl, stirring well to fully incorporate. The batter should be very wet. Stir in the cinnamon and nutmeg.

In a small bowl, toss the blueberries lightly with the confectioners' sugar, then fold them into the batter.

Grease a large baking dish or individual ramekins and pour in the batter. Dot the top of the batter with butter. Pour 1 to 2 inches of warm water into a large, deep baking sheet. Place the ramekins or baking dish on the baking sheet with the water. The water should go up about halfway on the ramekins or baking dish to ensure even cooking. Put in the oven and bake until nicely browned, about 45 minutes. Serve immediately.

Cold Winter Night Flourless Chocolate Cake

Makes one 10-inch round cake

If chocolate is your weakness, watch out for this dense cake! It is a perfect ending to any meal, and with only four main ingredients, it is at the top of my list for an effortless creation. It is also a wonderful dessert for people who might have wheat allergies, since no flour is needed. You should make it one day ahead, so plan accordingly. For extra chocolate decadence, make the Ganache with Panache (see page 163) and pour over the cake just before you serve it.

2 cups (4 sticks) unsalted butter

30 ounces semisweet chocolate

1 tablespoon vanilla, cognac, or raspberry liqueur

9 eggs, at room temperature

Preheat the oven to 400°F.

Using a double boiler over medium heat, combine the butter and the chocolate, stirring constantly until they are melted and well incorporated. Add the vanilla or liqueur and remove from the heat, allowing the mixture to cool a bit. In a separate bowl, whip the eggs until they have tripled in volume. Carefully fold one-third of the eggs into the chocolate mixture, then fold in the remainder.

Line a 10-inch springform pan with a circle of parchment paper, then spray the pan lightly with cooking spray. Cover the outside of the pan with foil to protect it from any water seeping in. Pour the batter into the pan and place the pan in an oven-safe dish with a few inches of hot water. Place in the oven and cook for approximately 18 minutes (the cake will still jiggle when done). Remove the cake from the oven and allow it to cool in the pan of water for another 15 to 20 minutes. Place the cake in the refrigerator overnight. For best flavor, allow the cake to come to room temperature prior to serving.

Susitna Apple Rosemary Sorbet

Makes 4 servings

This is one of those dishes that will make your guests think you must have spent hours working on it, but in reality it's quite easy to prepare. Let people think you slaved away—I won't tell if you don't! For a beautiful presentation, top with apples and rosemary.

3 cups apple juice

1 cup red wine (zinfandel works very well)

½ cup granulated sugar

Juice of 2 to 3 lemons (about ⅓ cup)

3 tablespoons finely chopped fresh rosemary

Combine the apple juice, wine, sugar, lemon juice, and rosemary in a saucepan. Cook the mixture over medium-low heat until the sugar is dissolved. Remove from the heat and allow to steep for about 15 minutes.

Strain the liquid through a cheesecloth into a freezer-safe container. Freeze until firm, at least 12 hours. Scoop the sorbet into individual chilled bowls and garnish with apple slices and rosemary.

Best of Anchorage Crème Brûlée

Makes 4 to 6 servings

Crème brûlée takes a little time, but the end result is worth it. It seems like every chef has their own version of this dish, though I truly believe mine is the best around! Enjoy it with a cup of espresso to bring out the vanilla flavor.

4 cups heavy cream

¾ cup granulated sugar, plus more for sprinkling

1 vanilla bean, split

4 egg yolks

Preheat the oven to 300°F.

In a heavy saucepan, whisk together the cream, sugar, and vanilla bean. Heat the mixture to 180°F and remove from the heat.

Put the egg yolks in a separate bowl and slowly pour a ladleful of the hot cream into the egg yolks. Repeat until the temperature of the yolks is comparable to that of the cream. Pour the yolk mixture into the remaining cream until well combined. Pour the mixture through a strainer and allow it to cool to room temperature.

Put 4 to 6 ramekins on a sheet pan, filling them two-thirds full with the brûlée mixture. Place the pan in the center of the oven and fill the pan half full with warm water. Bake for about 45 minutes, or until set. Cool.

Sprinkle the cooled brûlée generously with granulated sugar; raw sugar works very well. Using a small kitchen torch, caramelize the sugar. Serve immediately.

Harvest Pumpkin Crème Brûlée

Makes 4 to 6 servings

Crème brûlée originated in France and was first seen in Massialot's (the first chef of Louis XIV) cookbook in 1691. This is a wonderful alternative to the traditional crème brûlée, although I don't know how Massialot would have felt about such a change to his creation. A shoo-in dessert for any holiday.

> **4 cups heavy cream**
>
> **¾ cup granulated sugar, plus more for sprinkling**
>
> **1 vanilla bean, split**
>
> **4 egg yolks**
>
> **1 cup canned pumpkin puree**
>
> **1 teaspoon ground cinnamon**
>
> **Pinch ground cloves**
>
> **Pinch ground ginger**

Preheat the oven to 300°F.

In a heavy saucepan, whisk together the cream, sugar, and vanilla bean. Heat the cream mixture to 180°F and remove from the heat.

Put the egg yolks in a separate bowl and slowly pour a ladleful of the hot cream into the egg yolks. Repeat until the temperature of the yolks is comparable to that of the cream. Pour the yolk mixture into the remaining cream until well combined. Whisk in the pumpkin puree and the cinnamon, cloves, and ginger. Pour the mixture through a strainer and allow it to cool to room temperature.

Put 4 to 6 ramekins on a sheet pan, filling them two-thirds full with the brûlée mixture. Place the pan in the center of the oven and fill the pan half full with warm water. Bake for about 45 minutes, or until set. Cool.

Sprinkle generously with granulated sugar. Using a small kitchen torch, caramelize the sugar. Serve immediately.

Chocolate and Apricot Crepes

Makes 4 to 6 servings

The combination of chocolate and apricots in these crepes makes it a perfect dessert for any occasion. You can also substitute other fruit preserves, such as strawberry, or even marmalade.

Crepes

> **2 cups whole milk**
>
> **1 cup all-purpose flour**
>
> **2 eggs, beaten**
>
> **2 tablespoons unsalted butter, melted and slightly browned**
>
> **1 tablespoon finely grated orange peel**
>
> **1 tablespoon granulated sugar**
>
> **½ teaspoon vanilla**

Using an electric mixer, beat together the milk, flour, eggs, butter, orange peel, sugar, and vanilla. Mix well after each addition. Spray a crepe pan or a large non-stick skillet with a bit of cooking spray to prevent the crepes from sticking. Heat over medium heat.

Ladle in a spoonful of the batter, turning the pan to coat evenly (the layer should be thin). When the bottom is lightly browned, carefully flip the crepe with a spatula or your fingertips and cook the other side. Keep warm until ready to use.

Filling

8 ounces (1 cup) ricotta cheese (preferably whole milk)

¼ cup mascarpone cheese (2 ounces)

½ cup apricot preserves

½ cup bittersweet or semisweet chocolate (about 3 ounces), finely chopped

Ground coffee

Confectioners' sugar

Using an electric mixer, blend together the ricotta with the mascarpone until smooth. Mix in the preserves, stirring until incorporated but some chunks remain. Pour in the chocolate and mix until just blended.

Transfer the mixture to a pastry bag without a tip (a plastic bag with the corner cut off works fine too). Pipe the mixture into the crepes. Sprinkle the ends of the cheese filling with coffee. Sift confectioners' sugar over the crepes and serve immediately.

City Diner Pineapple Upside-Down Cake

Makes one 9-inch round cake

Pineapple upside-down cake has long been considered a classic American dessert. Thought to have originated back in the 1920s, it remains a much-loved comfort food today. This moist and delicious cake is a very popular dessert at City Diner. It is very easy to substitute other fruits in this cake. Try peaches, pears, or apples for a twist on the traditional.

1½ cups all-purpose flour

1½ teaspoons baking powder

½ teaspoon salt

½ teaspoon ground cinnamon

½ cup (1 stick) unsalted butter, softened

⅔ cup granulated sugar

2 large eggs

1 teaspoon vanilla

¾ cup whole milk

Topping (recipe follows)

Whipped cream or vanilla ice cream

Preheat the oven to 350°F.

In a large bowl sift together the flour, baking powder, salt, and cinnamon. Using an electric mixer, beat together the butter and sugar until light and fluffy, about 5 minutes. Mix in the eggs, one at a time, beating well after each addition. Pour in the vanilla, again mixing well. Alternately add portions of the flour mixture and milk, beginning and ending with the flour mixture and beating well after each addition.

Pour the batter into the pan containing the topping mixture, spreading it evenly. Place the cake in the middle of the oven and bake for 45 to 55 minutes, or until a tester comes out clean.

Let the cake cool in the pan on a rack for 15 minutes, run a thin knife around the edge, and invert the cake onto a plate. Serve at room temperature with whipped cream or vanilla ice cream.

Topping

¼ cup (½ stick) unsalted butter, melted

⅔ cup firmly packed light brown sugar

3 cups 1-inch chunks fresh pineapple (about 1 pineapple)

In a medium-size bowl, combine the butter and brown sugar until smooth. Spread the mixture evenly in a well-buttered 9-inch round cake pan. Pat the pineapple very dry with paper towels and arrange it evenly on the brown sugar mixture.

Winter Wonderland White Chocolate Cheesecake

Makes one 9-inch cheesecake

Can cheesecake be even richer and more decadent? Of course it can! The addition of white chocolate and Chambord creates a dessert that will wow your guests and satisfy any sweet tooth.

> **Four 8-ounce packages cream cheese**
>
> **1 cup granulated sugar**
>
> **2 tablespoons Chambord (raspberry liqueur)**
>
> **1 cup grated white chocolate (8 ounces)**
>
> **4 eggs, beaten**
>
> **Store-bought graham cracker or chocolate crust**

Preheat the oven to 325°F.

Whip the cream cheese until it is smooth. Add the sugar and continue mixing until well combined. Pour in the Chambord and the white chocolate. Add the eggs, one at a time, until each is incorporated.

Line a springform pan with the crust (a chocolate crust will make this dessert very rich). Carefully pour the cheesecake batter over the crust and bake for 30 minutes.

Turn off the oven and allow the cheesecake to sit in the oven for another 15 to 20 minutes, or until it sets. Serve with fresh raspberries and whipped cream.

Wild Blueberry Rhubarb Tarts

Makes 4 to 6 tarts

If there is one thing Alaska has an abundance of, it's our wonderful wild blueberries. Rhubarb is also quite prolific up here. It's easy to find a gardener who will share some of his or her excess, or you can just grow your own.

¾ cup cornmeal

2¼ cups all-purpose flour

1 scant teaspoon salt

1 cup (2 sticks) chilled unsalted butter, cut into small cubes

¾ cup cold water

1 cup rhubarb, rinsed, patted dry, and chopped

½ cup blueberries

¼ cup granulated sugar, plus more for sprinkling

1 teaspoon cornstarch

1 egg, beaten

Preheat the oven to 325°F.

In a large bowl, mix together the cornmeal, flour, and salt, then, using an electric mixer, slowly add the butter, about half a stick at a time. Pour in the cold water and mix by hand to form the dough (do not overmix). Refrigerate the dough for 2 hours or overnight.

Roll the dough out to ¼-inch thickness. Using a flat saucer as a guide, cut the dough into circles. In a small bowl, gently mix together the rhubarb, blueberries, sugar, and cornstarch. Scoop a small amount of the rhubarb mixture onto each disc and fold it over, pinching to seal. Brush the surface with egg and sprinkle it with granulated sugar.

Place the tarts on a baking sheet lightly sprayed with cooking spray and bake in the oven for 14 to 18 minutes until golden brown.

Index

About the Author

Chef Al Levinsohn was born in California and raised in the Seattle area before moving to Alaska. He began his culinary career working for Seattle-area hotels in the late seventies and was promoted to his first sous-chef position at age eighteen.

Al has worked in such legendary restaurants as the Alyeska Prince Hotel and Resort and the Glacier BrewHouse, where he developed the menu and kitchen setup of Anchorage's flagship brewpub.

In 2003, Chef Al's vision of owning his own restaurant came true with the opening of Kincaid Grill, which has become one of Anchorage's top restaurants. The year 2007 brought yet another dream realized with the opening of City Diner, a joint venture between Chef Al and Chef Jens Nannestad of Anchorage's Southside Bistro.

Throughout his career, Al has built up a list of accomplishments including five AAA Four Diamond Awards, multiple television appearances on the Food Network, and a guest chef spot at the James Beard House in New York City. He hosts his own cooking show, *What's Cookin'? with Chef Al*, that appears weekly on Alaska's KTUU.

Jody Ellis-Knapp is a freelance writer and lifetime Alaskan, currently making her home in Chugiak, just north of Anchorage. Her work has appeared in many local Anchorage publications, as well as national magazines across the United States.